April 2   113-116, 140-144   133 - 169
    16
    30 187-9   159-168 (MAY 7 - TEST)

may 14   214

Under the Advisory Editorship of
JACK M. WATSON
Dean, College-Conservatory of Music
of the University of Cincinnati

FUNDAMENTALS OF SIGHT SINGING AND EAR TRAINING

FUNDAMENTALS

OF

SIGHT SINGING

AND

EAR TRAINING

ARNOLD FISH

Juilliard School of Music

NORMAN LLOYD

Dean of the Conservatory of Music
Oberlin College

HARPER & ROW, PUBLISHERS
NEW YORK   EVANSTON   SAN FRANCISCO   LONDON

FUNDAMENTALS OF SIGHT SINGING AND
EAR TRAINING

Library of Congress Catalog Card Number: 64-12474
Standard Book Number: 06-042082-0

EDITOR'S INTRODUCTION

From a purely practical standpoint, a prime requisite for anyone entering the music profession is the ability to sight-read. With the high and varied demands on musicians today, efficient reading becomes all the more important. Yet the music teacher in school cannot afford the time to teach himself by a semi-rote process the music he is called upon to conduct or to teach to children; the would-be professional ensemble performer who is not a skillful reader has little chance of employment in a substantial musical organization; even the unusually talented soloist who is not a "fast study" carries a built-in handicap that may keep him on the concert or operatic sidelines.

From a musical standpoint, training in sight singing can be training in musicianship. (It can also be mechanical drill.) The French long ago recognized this, and as a result, solfège became the foundation of the curricula of the *Conservatoire*. Others have followed the same line. Zoltán Kodály, for example, considers the skill so important that he has spent years developing a system for teaching school children of Hungary to sing at sight.

In the United States, in spite of the fact that the history of music in the public schools has often revolved around the issue of sight reading *vs.* rote singing, we have, with notable exceptions, tended to "let nature take its course." Only those students with marked flair and motivation have become proficient readers. Fortunately, at least at the higher education level, the situation seems to be changing. Several new sight-singing texts have appeared and there is evidence that music departments are increasingly concerned over this aspect of the curriculum.

For several years two members of the Juilliard School of Music faculty have experimented in their classes with techniques and materials for teaching sight singing and ear training. They have evolved a program of instruction that has successfully met the pragmatic criterion of "does it work?" The present text is the first and more elementary part of the program. (The second textbook is now in preparation.)

Messrs. Fish and Lloyd have brought varied backgrounds to their experimentation. Both are composers and performing musicians, fully aware of the high standards of practical musicianship that today's professionals must meet. Both have been administrators and have dealt with over-all curricular matters. One majored in composition and, at the graduate level, musicology; the other was trained as a public school music teacher and later specialized in composition and piano. Their collective teaching experience includes music classes for elementary education majors, dance majors, liberal arts students, and children; courses for music education majors; and, of course, their work with professional students at Juilliard.

Fish and Lloyd are mature composers, as the exercises attest. They have composed exercises to present technical problems when these problems were not to be found in pedagogically advantageous form in existing music, as did Bach, and others. They have prescribed drill. But musicians have known all along that one cannot develop technique without drill; the preponderance of psychologists who specialize in the psychology of learning, according to Ernest Hilgard, agree that drill—or repetitive practice, as he calls it—is essential for skill development.

With sight singing and ear training, there is a big difference between knowledge and performance. To know that a particular melodic figure outlines an augmented triad and is a triplet rhythmically is one thing; to conceive it mentally and perform it at sight in an ongoing musical context is another. Recognizing this difference, the authors have isolated pitch and rhythmic problems and treated them individually, providing sufficient drill material to bring them to a reliable level of performance. They have provided a precisely graded learning program built around these pitch and rhythmic problems with their performance, *not* knowledge of them, the basis of organization. The authors have taken for granted the fact that college and conservatory students have had some prior musical experience and are relatively mature and motivated to learn. In the instructional material there is no talking down; there is no exhortation.

In sum, the program treats sight singing and ear training in both creative musicianship and intellectual musicianship. Students are taught to hear mentally what they see, as well as to reproduce it with their voices; they are taught to understand what they see and hear, and to think and create organized patterns of musical sound; they are taught to perceive, respond to, and reproduce rhythm as a dynamic, organic entity, not merely as a complex mathematico-metrical phenomenon; they are taught part-singing in two, three, and four parts. And through parallel and closely integrated experience with aesthetically appealing music of various periods, they are led to become more sensitive to stylistic and expressive values in music.

Yet with all its precision and definiteness, the program is flexible and readily adjustable to a variety of curricular patterns and adaptable to the musical level and schedule of classes.

Jack M. Watson

FOREWORD

This book has been written for beginning students of sight singing and ear training. Every competent musician must be able to read with fluency and accuracy the tonal and rhythmic language of music, and because *Fundamentals of Sight Singing and Ear Training* has been designed expressly to develop the skills necessary for sight reading, the book addresses itself to the needs of all serious music students—singers and instrumentalists, as well as students of composition, conducting, music education, and musicology—who have not yet acquired these skills.

The material is arranged in a series of carefully graded units, each unit dealing with basic aspects of rhythm and pitch. Within each unit musical problems are presented and analyzed; drills specific to each problem are given, together with instructions as to the performance of these drills; finally, examples of the problems in music of various periods and styles incorporate the elements of each unit into the context of music literature.

Special attention is given to rhythmic problems which, in our opinion, comprise the most neglected area of music education. The student who is unsure rhythmically is unsure musically.

Since the content of this book parallels much of the material usually covered in first-year theory courses, it can be used effectively in conjunction with a theory text or syllabus. Its organization into units (instead of class lessons) makes it a flexible tool in the hands of the teacher, who can adjust it to his own lesson plans according to the ability and background of his students and to the exigencies of the course schedule.

The material in the text is, in a way, a synthesis of our own approaches to sight singing and ear training with students of various levels and orientations—from professional musicians to students in conservatories, teachers colleges, liberal arts colleges, adult education programs, and preparatory institutions.

The technique of sight reading—intelligent musical analysis on the practical level of performance—is an essential ingredient of musicianship. It is from this point of view and toward the achievement of this end that *Fundamentals of Sight Singing and Ear Training* has been written.

Arnold Fish
Norman Lloyd

vii

NOTES TO THE TEACHER

With this book, as with any textbook, the creative teacher is an important collaborator. By supplementing the text with additional facts, new drills, and relevant ideas, the teacher will not only enrich the musical background of his students, but will also stimulate them into recognizing the direct and essential relationship which exists between the mastery of certain skills and the requirements of musicianship. If this relationship can be made clear by the teacher, the class will be relieved of that feeling of plodding which all too often blights the spirits of creative students obliged to master practical skills.

In using the materials in this book with our own students, we have discovered some teaching techniques that have proved particularly effective, and we are passing them on to you as suggestions. (You will no doubt want to modify some and elaborate upon others.)

1. Most of the ear-training exercises call for original work by students. As preparation for these assignments, it is helpful to analyze a few melodies, calling attention to such organizing principles and devices as repetition of ideas, logical rhythmic progressions, climax tones that give a sense of direction to melodies, and so forth.

2. We suggest that when dictating intervals you give variety to the drills. Use all registers of the piano. Play some intervals slowly, others rapidly. Hold some harmonic intervals, play others staccato. Change the direction of intervals so that students become used to singing and identifying intervals from high to low as well as from low to high. As students become more familiar with intervals, play tones more than an octave apart, and so on.

3. "Negative ear training," or the intentional inclusion of mistakes in the playing of a notated melody, has proven to be a particularly fruitful teaching device. It is not only an instructive and interesting method of conducting ear-training sessions, but it sharpens the wits and the musical senses of individual students, as well as keeps the class on its collective toes. Here is one way of handling "negative ear training":

Write a melody on the board. Play it with several incorrect notes (in pitch or rhythm). The class is to tell which notes were changed, and, if possible, what notes were played instead of the notated ones. In more advanced work this can be done with short piano pieces.

For students preparing to teach—privately or in classes—"negative ear training" is especially important.

4. An interesting and useful technique is what we call "silent reading." On the signal "stop," the performers stop singing aloud but con-

tinue to read the melody silently. On the signal "sing," they resume
singing aloud. The same procedure may be used with rhythmic exercises.

5. It is not necessary for an exercise to be completed before beginning the next, we discovered. Part of one exercise might be studied in
class and the remainder assigned as homework. In some cases, the
last few melodies or studies within an exercise are rather difficult.
They are, in a sense, challenges for the superior students. Weak students may have to work quite hard to perform these studies even at a
moderate rate of speed.

6. You may wish to supplement the material in this book with solo
or choral works. Collections of folk songs are excellent for this purpose.
Effective, too, are symphonic works by Mozart and Haydn, which may
be clapped, and whole movements of which may be used as rhythmic
studies.

NOTES TO THE STUDENT

Sight singing is a skill that demands practice and concentration. Studies should never be done as mechanical drills, but always as an aspect of the art of music. Ear training, in essence, means becoming aware of and identifying sounds that you have heard thousands of times, and learning to notate them. Learning to sight read means learning to see a note, not just as an isolated symbol, but as a *sound* that is a part of a group of sounds making up a phrase or a part of a total work.

Here are some points that will help you as you study the material in this book:

1. Do each rhythmic and melodic study in its entirety. *Do not stop to make corrections*. Stopping breaks the flow of rhythm and leads to a halting and insecure performance. When you make mistakes, go back and isolate them; practice the weak spots; then perform the entire study correctly several times before moving to the next.

2. Use the following as a general procedure for each study:

   a) Glance through the entire study before attempting to perform it. Look for new rhythmic or melodic problems. Make a mental note of those that might cause trouble and analyze them in relation to the surrounding material.

   b) Always look ahead. Do not keep your eyes on the notes you are performing, but keep them on those that lie ahead.

   c) Try to read groups of notes as patterns rather than as a series of individual notes—as you read words and phrases in a book. Reading music note by note is like reading a story letter by letter.

   d) Choose a moderate tempo, unless a tempo mark is given. Repeat each study at various tempos.

   e) Determine the purpose of each study—the musical problem being treated. Relate this problem to the music you are studying on your instrument or at your voice lesson.

3. When the melody is in the bass, women should sing their part in their own range; when it is in the treble, men should sing their part in their range. When the melody ranges high, it is often easier for men to sing with a light tone—*mezzo voce*—than in full voice.

4. Locate the first tone of each study on the piano, pitch pipe, et cetera. However, do *not* play through a study on the piano or any other instrument except where specifically indicated. Using an instrument will lead merely to rote memorization and will impede your learning of sight-singing skills.

5. Don't allow lack of practice facilities to interfere with your progress in ear training. One technique that calls for no facilities (other than pencil and paper) is to notate familiar folk songs, hymn tunes, popular songs, or "singing commercials." You can practice this in class or out. After notating a few phrases or an entire piece, check your version either by performing it yourself or having a classmate perform it. Another technique is this: As you listen to music, practice visualizing it in musical notation; later, check your version against the printed score, if a score is available.

6. If you have problems with rhythm, try singing and clapping the rhythmic patterns of various instrumental parts in symphonic works by Haydn and Mozart.

7. Remember, the important thing is that you practice sight reading often and regularly.

CONTENTS

FUNDAMENTALS OF SIGHT SINGING AND EAR TRAINING

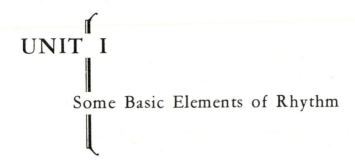

UNIT I

Some Basic Elements of Rhythm

Music is an art directly dependent upon the dimension of time. Like drama and dance, music is a time art; it *exists* in time. Music is also *organized* in time, and the organizing phenomenon is called "rhythm," which comes from the Greek *rhythmos* meaning "continuity" or "flow." *Rhythm,* therefore, is a broad concept and an all-inclusive one covering everything having to do with the temporal aspect of music. It includes such subordinate concepts as "pulse," "tempo," "note values," "rhythmic patterns," "meter," and, in a sense, even "phrase" and "period." (An understanding of rhythm is dependent upon the recognition of time relationships—of one pulse to another, one phrase to another, or of one large section of a composition to another large section. In this sense, an understanding of rhythm is basic to an understanding of musical form.)

Of all rhythmic elements, the most fundamental is *pulse.*

Exercise I. Pulse and Tempo

1. Sing several well-known songs, such as "America" or "Deck the Halls" and, while singing, clap or tap a steady beat in time with the music. (Most music has such a steady, continuous, regular "recurring pulse" or "fundamental beat." Pulse is a sense of marking time; it may be predominant and clearly heard, as in a march, or subtle and merely felt, as in a slow movement of a symphony.)

2. Listen to some of the more complex melodies in this book, while the instructor or a member of the class plays them, and clap or tap the pulse.

3. Listen to recordings (or live performances) of court dance forms such as allemandes, courantes, sarabandes, minuets, and gigues in Bach's French and English suites. Notice how the pulses of different dances move at different rates of speed. (The rate of speed at which a musical work is performed is referred to as its *tempo*.)

1

Exercise II. One-pulse and Two-pulse Relationships

1. Set up a basic pulse by tapping on a hard surface, such as a desk or a book. Continue tapping while intoning one note for every two taps. Reverse the procedure by intoning the pulse and tapping one note for every two pulses.

2. Tap the basic pulse with the left hand while tapping one note in the right hand to every two pulses. On a given signal, such as "change," reverse the duties of the two hands.

In notation, the pulse can be any type of note (the whole note is usually avoided as the pulse note.) Depending on which note is chosen as the pulse note, the note that lasts for two pulses will be the next larger type of note. For example, if the pulse note is a ♩ then o is equal to two pulses.

Exercise III. Rhythmic Studies

Perform the material given below in the following manner:

1. Tap the pulse while intoning the exercise on a neutral syllable (ta, da, la.) *Be sure to give each note its full value* and feel the pulse in your body while clapping the patterns.

2. Tap the pattern with each hand separately.

3. Tap the pattern with alternating hands.

(a) Patterns where ♩ = one pulse, and o = two pulses.

(b) Patterns where ♩ = one pulse, ♩ = two pulses.

(c) Patterns where ♪ = one pulse, ♩ = two pulses. (Note that groups of
eighth notes are often connected by a beam: ♫ = ♪ ♪)

(d) Patterns where ♪ = one pulse, ♩ = two pulses. (Note that groups of two sixteenth notes are often connected by a double beam:

Exercise IV. Ear Training

Each student should make up short rhythmic patterns of six to ten notes in length, similar to the patterns in Exercise III, and dictate his patterns to the class, first announcing the value of the pulse note. The patterns may be sung, tapped, or played on the piano. Each student should dictate his pattern three times, pausing between the repetitions. The class should first sing or tap the pattern until it is memorized. Then each student should write the pattern.

The following technique is sometimes helpful in rhythmic dictation:

1. Horizontal strokes are used to indicate the sounds that are articu-lated; longer strokes are used to indicate longer note values:

— — —— —— — — — —— —

2. Vertical strokes are written under the horizontal ones to show the number of pulses given to each note:

| | || || | | | | |||

3. Finally, the actual notes are written:

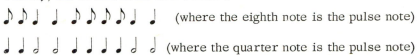 (where the eighth note is the pulse note)

(where the quarter note is the pulse note)

Exercise V. Rhythmic Studies

Perform this exercise in the following manner:

1. Set the tempo of the pulse note.

2. Intone the pattern while clapping the pulse (say: ta, ta, ta, etc.)

3. Clap the pattern while intoning the pulse (say: beat, beat, beat, etc.)

4. Tap the pattern with the right hand, the pulse with the left hand.

5. Tap the pattern with the left hand, the pulse with the right hand.

(a) Patterns where ♩ = one pulse.

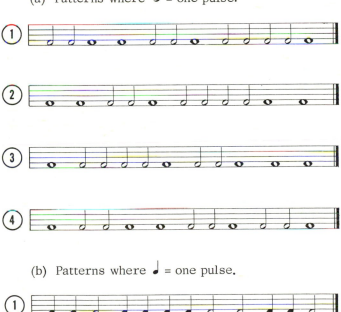

(b) Patterns where ♩ = one pulse.

(c) Patterns where ♪ = one pulse.

(d) Patterns where ♪ = one pulse.

Exercise VI. Rhythmic Studies in Two Voices

Perform the two-part material of this exercise in the following manner:

1. Half the class intones the upper part while the other half claps the lower part. Reverse the parts. Perform as duets with one student to each part.

2. Tap the upper part with the right hand, the lower part with the left.

3. Intone the upper part while clapping the lower. Reverse parts.

4. Do each exercise several times.

(a) Patterns where 𝅗𝅥 = one pulse.

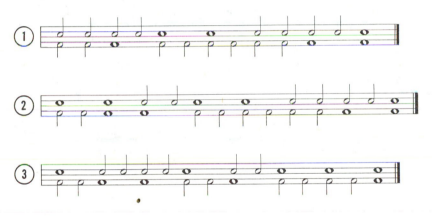

(b) Patterns where ♩ = one pulse.

(c) Patterns where ♪ = one pulse.

(d) Patterns where ♪ = one pulse.

Exercise VII. Rhythmic Canons

The patterns given below will work as two-voice canons. (A canon is a compositional device in which one or more voices delay their entries before imitating the first, or leading, voice.)

Perform each exercise in unison. Then, with the class divided into two groups, the first group begins to sing, while the second group waits the indicated number of pulses. The second group then imitates what the first group has done. For example, the pattern ♩♩ ♩ ♩♩♩♩♩♩♩♩♩ is to be performed:

Perform the canons, first clapping, then intoning the notes. Switch parts so that each group gets a chance to lead.

1. Second group waits four pulses (eighth note is the pulse note).

2. Second group waits three pulses (quarter note is the pulse note).

3. Second group waits two pulses (quarter note is the pulse note)

4. Second group waits four pulses (quarter note is the pulse note).

5. Second group waits two pulses (half note is the pulse note),

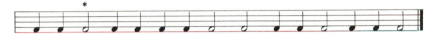

Exercise VIII.   Ear Training

This· exercise is to be done with one student, at the piano, as the leader. (The improvized rhythmic pattern can be played on one tone.) The leader sets a moderate pulse by playing a group of four steady beats. Next he plays a series of short patterns, each of which adds up to four pulses (using one-pulse and two-pulse values). The class waits four pulses before imitating the leader's first pattern.

The exercise should continue for six to eight patterns with the class clapping one pattern while listening to the next.

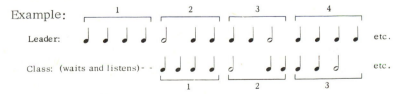

UNIT II

Basic Pitch Relationships; Stepwise Melodies in the Major Scale

The simplest form of pitch relationship is that found between adjacent tones of the major scale pattern. There is only one *major* scale pattern. It can be built above any *tonic,* or *keynote.* The tonic is the home base toward which most sounds in a composition gravitate. This tendency to feel one tone as "home" is generally referred to as *tonality* or *key feeling.* In tonal music almost every melody ultimately ends on the tonic of the scale in which the melody is written.

The smallest musical interval—the *minor second,* or *half step*—is found between the third and fourth and the seventh and eighth tones of the major scale. The *major second,* or *whole step,* is found between the other adjacent scale degrees:

Exercise I. Preparatory Practice for Stepwise Studies

Sing the following major scale-degree patterns. Start on various tonics, always maintaining an even pulse. (The musical example shows the beginning of the exercise in the key of C major.)

1-2-1
1-2-3-2-1
1-2-3-4-3-2-1
1-2-3-4-5-4-3-2-1
1-2-3-4-5-6-5-4-3-2-1
1-2-3-4-5-6-7-6-5-4-3-2-1
1-2-3-4-5-6-7-8-7-6-5-4-3-2-1

Exercise II. Stepwise Studies in the Major Scale

Scan each melody before singing. Note the rise and fall in the melodic line. Aim to develop an awareness of how each tone relates to its adjacent tone and to the tonic and be prepared to sing the tonic at any time. Never lose a sense of where "home" is, and, as always in reading music, *look ahead !*

Sing the material in this exercise in several ways, always maintaining an even pulse:

1. Use the letter names of notes: C-D-E, etc.

2. Use conventional syllables: do-re-mi, etc.

3. Think the scale degree of each tone (all melodies in this exercise are in C major). Sing the melodies on scale numbers (C is 1, D is 2, etc.).

4. Use a neutral syllable: la, lu, etc.

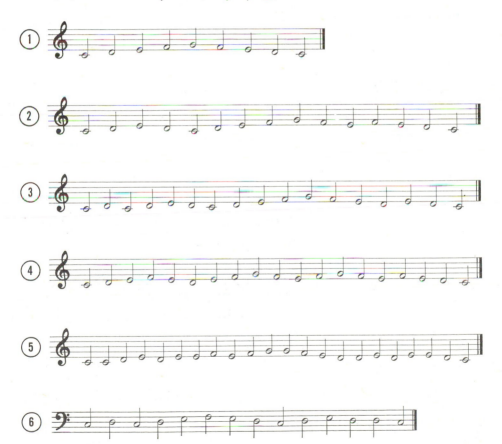

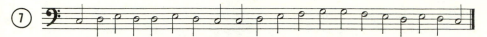

5. Transpose the melodic patterns to the keys of D major and B♭ major. Sing, using the letter names of the new keys.

Exercise III.   Preparatory Practice for Melodies That Lie Below the Tonic

When melodies consistently lie below the tonic it is usually easier to think of the tonic tone as scale number 8, rather than scale number 1.

Sing the following patterns starting on various tonics. Maintain an even pulse. (The musical example shows the beginning of the exercise in C major.)

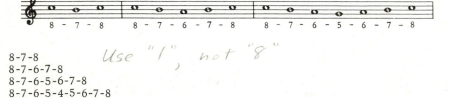

8 - 7 - 8   8 - 7 - 6 - 7 - 8   8 - 7 - 6 - 5 - 6 - 7 - 8

8-7-8   *Use "1", not "8"*
8-7-6-7-8
8-7-6-5-6-7-8
8-7-6-5-4-5-6-7-8
8-7-6-5-4-3-4-5-6-7-8
8-7-6-5-4-3-2-3-4-5-6-7-8
8-7-6-5-4-3-2-1-2-3-4-5-6-7-8

Exercise IV.   Stepwise Studies in the Major Scale, Moving Above and Below the Tonic

Sing the following studies on letter names, scale-degree numbers, and syllables.

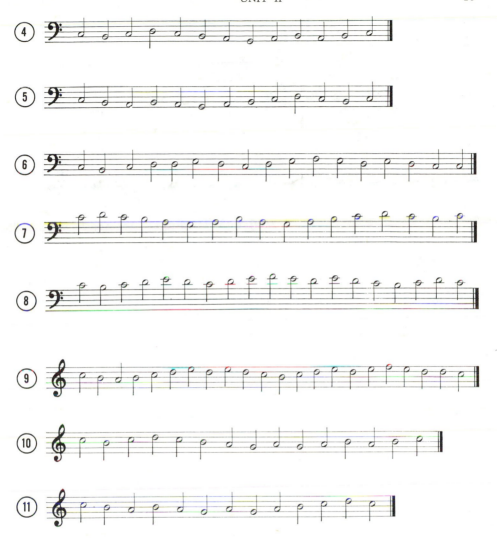

Exercise V. Studies in C♯ and C♭ Major

Perform the melodies given below in a manner similar to those in Exercise IV. Note that the scales of C♯ major (seven sharps) and C♭ major (seven flats) look, without their key signatures, exactly like the scale of C major.

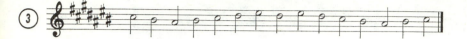

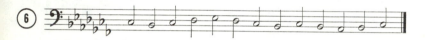

Exercise VI. Ear Training

Make up melodic lines of eight to twelve tones that move by step and in an even pulse. Let each melody start and end on the tonic of C major. Sing or play each melody several times for the rest of the class. The class is then to sing the melody and notate it.

Exercise VII. Melodic Studies Using One- and Two-pulse Notes

The melodies in this exercise combine problems of pitch and rhythm. Determine the pulse before singing each melody and be sure to maintain each tone for its full value. Sing on letter names, scale-degree numbers, and syllables.

(a) ♩ = one pulse, 𝅝 = two pulses

(b) ♩ = one pulse, ♩. = two pulses

(c)   ♪ = one pulse,   ♩ = two pulses

(d)   ♪ = one pulse,   ♪ = two pulses

Exercise VIII. Melodies Over Rhythmic Ostinatos

In each of the following studies the lower voice has a rhythmic *ostinato* (a reiterated pattern) indicated by the bracket (└────┘).

1. The class should be divided into two groups, one group singing the melody while the other group sings or claps the ostinato rhythmic pattern. (This may be performed by two soloists as well as by two groups.)

2. Each person sings the melody while tapping the ostinato pattern.

(a) 𝅗𝅥 = one pulse

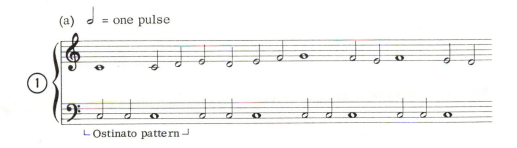

└ Ostinato pattern ┘

(b) 𝅘𝅥 = one pulse

(c) ♪ = one pulse

Exercise IX. Two-voice Melodic Studies

The following two-part studies require two performers (or two groups). They may also be practiced by singing one part and playing the other. Sing each study on letter names, scale-degree numbers, and syllables.

(a)   ♩ = one pulse

(b)   ♩ = one pulse

(c)   ♪ = one pulse

Exercise X. Ear Training

Make up short stepwise melodies using one- and two-pulse note values. Begin and end on the tonic and keep the melodies within a small range. Sing or play your melody to the rest of the class. After several repetitions the class should be able to sing back the melody, while imitating its rise or fall by motions of the hand. The class then notates the melody.

Exercise XI. Drills on Major and Minor Seconds

1. Sing minor seconds above given piano tones. (Think of the sound of scale degrees 7-8.)

2. Sing minor seconds below given piano tones. (Think scale degrees 8-7.)

3. Sing major seconds above given piano tones. (Think of the sound of scale degrees 1-2.)

4. Sing major seconds below given piano tones. (Think scale degrees 2-1.)

5. Sing short "chains" of major and minor seconds, such as:

   (a) Minor second, major second, above a tone (like scale degrees 7-8-2). See example below.

   (b) Major second, major second, below a tone (like scale degrees 3-2-1)

   (c) Minor second, major second, major second, below a tone (like scale degrees 8-7-6-5)

   Etc.

   Example of a "chain" of seconds

   (The last tone of the pattern becomes the first tone of the next pattern.)

   (The second tone of the pattern becomes the first tone of the next pattern)

6. Identify major and minor seconds when played on the piano harmonically (together) and melodically (in succession).

UNIT III

Major and Minor Thirds in the Major Scale; Plainsong

Sing the first two phrases of "Frère Jacques," starting on C. Imitate the rise and fall of the melodic line by raising and lowering your right hand. Note that in the first phrase the second and third tones move up smoothly from the tonic by step, and the third tone falls back to the tonic in a small leap. This leap, from E down to C, is called an interval of a *major third*. A major third consists of two whole steps: C-D, D-E. (The direction of a leap does not matter in measuring intervals. C to E, going up, is the same size as E to C, coming down.)

In the second phrase of "Frère Jacques" there is another third: G down to E. This is a *minor third*. It consists of a step and a half: E-F, F-G.

Exercise I. Melodic Studies Using Major and Minor Thirds

Sing and study the sequential patterns given below.

1. Analyze the grouping of the notes.

2. Sing the first and second examples, using numbers to represent the scale degrees.

In the first two examples note the three-tone figures that cover the distance of a major third, observing as well those that cover the distance of a minor third. There are major thirds between which scale degrees? There are minor thirds between which scale degrees?

3. Sing examples 3, 4, 5, and 6 on scale numbers. Note whether the thirds are major or minor.

If there is difficulty in singing some of the thirds in tune, mentally insert the scale tone that falls between the two given tones. In this way the problem becomes one of merely thinking scale steps. Then proceed to attempt the direct leap of the third.

Exercise II. Melodies Combining Stepwise Movement and Leaps of Major and Minor Thirds

1. Sing the melody on scale-degree numbers.

2. Sing the melodies using conventional syllables (do-re-mi, etc.).

3. Sing the melodies using neutral syllables (la, lu, etc.).

♩ = one pulse

(10)

(11)

(12)

(13)

(14)

(15)

(16)

(17)

Gb major

1   2   3   2   etc.

F# major

1   2   3   1   etc.

Exercise III. Drills on Major and Minor Seconds, Major and Minor Thirds

1. Sing major thirds above given piano tones. (Think of scale degrees 1-3.)

2. Sing major thirds below given piano tones. (Think of scale degrees 3-1.)

3. Sing minor thirds above given piano tones. (Think of scale degrees 2-4, 3-5, or 6-8.)

4. Sing minor thirds below given piano tones. (Think of scale degrees 8-6, 5-3, or 4-2.)

The above exercises can be sung in a rhythmic pattern: Give the tone on the first pulse; then the class matches that tone on the second pulse, sings the specified interval on the third pulse, and holds the new tone through the fourth pulse. See the example below:

5. Sing short "chains" of seconds and thirds, such as:

   (a) Major third up, minor second down (like scale degrees 1-3-2).

   (b) Minor third below given tone, major second up, minor second up (like scale degrees 8-6-7-8).

   (c) Minor third above given tone, minor second down, major third down (like scale degrees 2-4-3-1).

6. Identify major and minor seconds, major and minor thirds when played on the piano harmonically (together) and melodically (in succession) from high to low or low to high. (Intervals should be dictated in various registers of the piano, at varying speeds, and with various touches—staccato, legato, etc.)

Exercise IV. Ear Training

Invent short major-scale melodic patterns similar to those in Exercise II. Each melody should contain stepwise motion and some skips of major and minor thirds. Use one-pulse or two-pulse note values in rhythm.

1. Each student plays or sings his melody three times, after announcing the key to the rest of the class.

2. After the third hearing, the class sings the pattern once or twice.

3. The class members write the melody and check their versions against the correct version written on the blackboard by the student-composer of the melody.

Exercise V. Singing Major and Minor Thirds, Placing Them in Key Relationships

The first tone in each of the following is to be played on the piano.

1. Sing the given tone and a major third below it. Call the tones 6-4 of a major scale and sing down the scale: 6-4-5-4-3-2-1.

2. Sing the given tone and a major third above it. Call the tones 5-7 of a major scale and sing 5-7-8 of the scale.

3. Sing the given tone and a minor third above it. Call the tones 2-4 of a major scale and sing 2-4-3-2-1 of that scale.

4. Sing the given tone and a minor third below it. Call the tones 5-3 of a major scale and sing 5-3-2-1 of that scale.

5. Sing the given tone and a minor third below it. Call the tones 8-6 of a major scale and sing 8-6-7-8 of that scale.

6. Sing the given tone and a minor third below it. Call the tones 2-7 of a major scale and sing 2-7-8-3-2-1 of that scale.
(1)

Exercise VI. Melodies from Gregorian Chants, Using Major and Minor Seconds and Major and Minor Thirds

The melodies given below were selected from the vast body of Roman Catholic liturgical songs known as Gregorian chants or plainsongs.

These medieval songs are generally interpreted with notes having the rhythmic values of one or two pulses. There is no regular accent; rather there is a sense of flow which continues gracefully from the beginning to the end of each phrase. (The end of each phrase is indicated by a vertical line drawn partially or completely through the staff. At that point a breath is to be taken.)

Many Gregorian chants are based on the medieval church scales known as *modes*. The chants in this exercise do not, however, offer any complexities from this standpoint. Each melody can be analyzed as if it were in the major scale of its beginning and ending tones.

REMINDERS

Always have the tonic in mind as the melody is being sung.

Glance through the entire melody. Be particularly aware of the types of thirds and seconds to be sung. If there is uncertainty when singing the leap of a third, mentally insert the scale tone which lies between the tones of the third.

Do not stop to make corrections. Start at a moderate tempo, and repeat at a faster tempo.

Be sure to give each tone its full time duration.

Sing the chants in the following ways: (a) without text, on letter names or syllables, (b) with text.

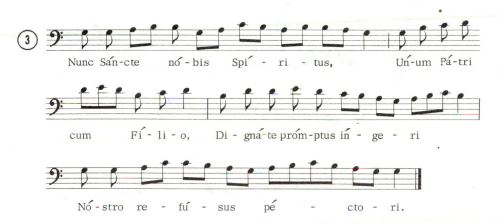

③ Nunc Sán-cte nó-bis Spí-ri-tus, Un-um Pá-tri

cum Fí-li-o, Di-gná-te próm-ptus in-ge-ri

Nó-stro re-fú-sus pé - cto-ri.

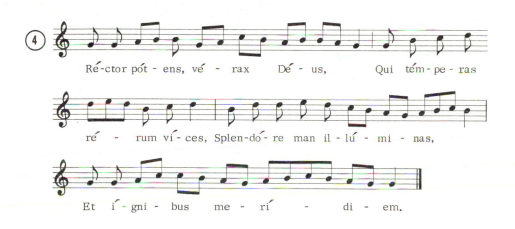

④ Ré-ctor pót-ens, vé-rax Dé-us, Qui tém-pe-ras

ré - rum ví-ces, Splen-dó-re man il-lú-mi-nas,

Et í-gni-bus me-rí - di-em.

⑤ Sur-réx-it Dó-mi-nus vé-re: Al-le-lú-ia, al-le-lú-ia

Et ap-pá-ru-it Si-mó-ni. Gló-ri-a Pá-tri, et Fí-li-o,

et Spi-rí-tu-i Sán-cto

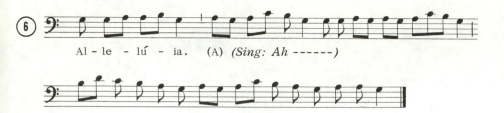

6 Al – le – lú – ia. (A) *(Sing: Ah ------)*

7 Má-ne-ant in vó – bis fí-des, spes, cá – ri – tas, trí – a

haec: má-jor aú-tem hó – rem est cá – ri – tas.

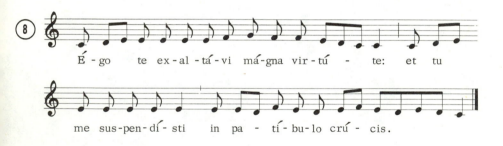

8 É – go te ex-al-tá-vi má-gna vir-tú – te: et tu

me sus-pen-dí-sti in pa – tí-bu-lo crú – cis.

9 Dó-mi-ne con – vér – te-re, et é – ri – pe

á – ni-mam mé – am: sál-vum me fac pró – pter

mi-se – ri-cór-di-am tú – am.

10. De frú-ctu ó-per-um tu -ó-rum Dó-mi-ne, sa-ti - á - bi-tur tér - ra: ut ed -ú - cas pá-nem de tér - ra et ví - num lae-tí - fi - cet cor hó - mi - nis: ut ex-hí - la - ret fá - ci-em in ó - le - o, et pá - nis cor hó - mi - nis con-fír - met.

UNIT IV

Meter; Elementary Conducting; Rhythmic Ratios of Three to One and Four to One; Melodies Beginning on Tones Other Than the Tonic; the Alto Clef

Meter is the grouping together of rhythmic pulses by means of regular, or fairly regular, accents or stresses. The basic meters, from which all others are derived, are those consisting of two pulses or three pulses. In *duple meter* there is a feeling of emphasis, or accent, on alternate pulses: 1 2 1 2 1 2. In *triple meter* the accent is felt every three pulses: 1 2 3   1 2 3   1 2 3 . *Quadruple meter* is a combination of two two-pulse measures, with a lesser accent on the third beat of each four-beat unit: 1 2 3 4   1 2 3 4   1 2 3 4

Bar lines are used to mark off the beginning of each metric group or measure. The first accented pulse of each group is called the *measure accent. Time signatures,* $\frac{2}{4}, \frac{3}{8}, \frac{3}{2}, \frac{4}{4}$, etc., are placed at the beginning of a musical composition. The lower figure of the time signature indicates the pulse note. The upper figure tells the number of pulses in each measure. When listening to music there is usually no way of telling which type of note is the pulse note, All that can be known is the number of pulses per measure. The composer decides whether his pulse note will be a half note, a quarter note, or an eighth note. (The quarter note is the most usual pulse note.)

Exercise I. Finding the Meter of a Composition

By means of recordings or live performance on the piano, listen to music of many different types: Strauss waltzes; Sousa marches; folk songs; movements from symphonic and chamber music works by Mozart, Haydn, and Beethoven; short piano works by Mendelssohn, Chopin, Schumann, and Brahms; court dance forms such as pavanes, galliards, allemandes, courantes, minuets, and sarabandes.

1. Tap the basic pulse of the composition.

2. Find the measure accent, thus determining the meter of the composition.

3. Clap the pulse, emphasizing the measure accent.

In many contemporary compositions, as well as some folk songs and certain dramatic works, the music shifts from one meter to another. In such a case a new time signature is used each time the meter changes: $\frac{2}{4}$ ♩ ♩ | ♩ ♩ |$\frac{3}{4}$ ♩ ♩ ♩ |$\frac{2}{4}$ ♩ ♩ etc.

Exercise II. Practice in Conducting Basic Meters

The primary duty of a conductor is to keep a group of singers or instrumentalists together. This is done by means of conventional hand or baton movements which outline the meter of a musical composition. Generally the first beat of a measure is indicated by a downward motion and the final beat of a measure by an upward motion: Ex. 1a. In actual performance the first downbeat is preceded by a short upward preparatory motion as if a singer were taking a breath. Thereafter the hand or baton moves in a flowing manner, as in Ex. 1b. The dotted lines indicate the "follow through" motion which takes up all the time from beat to beat. Each beat must have a definite ending so that there is no confusion in the minds of those following the conductor. While you practice the following conducting patterns with the right hand let that hand hit the outstretched palm of your left hand to get the feel of the "bottom" of the beat and the resultant bounce.

Example 1a shows the basic beat direction of *duple meter*. Example 1b shows the pattern traced by the hand.

Example 2a shows the basic beat direction of *triple meter*. Example 2b shows the pattern traced by the hand.

Example 3a shows the basic beat direction of *quadruple meter*. Example 3b shows the pattern traced by the hand.

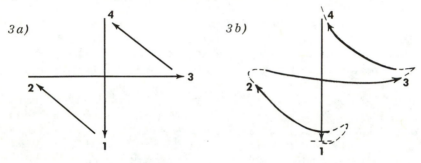

1. Practice the conducting patterns at various tempos until they become smooth, graceful, and almost automatic. Avoid conducting in such a manner that the beat is either too rigid or too loose. Notice that at a rapid tempo the size of the movement must be smaller than when the tempo is slow. Keep the beat at shoulder height.

2. Sing several well-known songs—such as "America," "Alouette," or "Old Folks at Home." Find the meter of each song and conduct while singing.

The material in Exercises III and IV below presents rhythmic relationships of three to one and four to one.

In a three-to-one-ratio, a dotted note must be used. A dot placed after a note increases the value of that note by one half: $\circ \cdot = \circ + \mathcal{J}$, $\mathcal{J} \cdot = \mathcal{J} + \mathcal{J}$, $\mathcal{J} \cdot = \mathcal{J} + \mathcal{J}$ etc. Therefore, any dotted note equals three of the next smaller type of note: $\circ \cdot = \mathcal{J} \ \mathcal{J} \ \mathcal{J}$, $\mathcal{J} \cdot = \mathcal{J} \ \mathcal{J} \ \mathcal{J}$, $\mathcal{J} \cdot = \mathcal{J} \ \mathcal{J} \ \mathcal{J}$ etc.

In a four-to-one ratio, the following relationships are found:

$\circ = \mathcal{J} \ \mathcal{J} \ \mathcal{J} \ \mathcal{J}$, $\mathcal{J} = \mathcal{J} \ \mathcal{J} \ \mathcal{J} \ \mathcal{J}$, $\mathcal{J} = \mathcal{J} \ \mathcal{J} \ \mathcal{J} \ \mathcal{J}$, $\mathcal{J} = \mathcal{J} \ \mathcal{J} \ \mathcal{J} \ \mathcal{J}$

Exercise III. Drills Using Three-to-one and Four-to-one Ratios

Perform the drills below as follows:

1. Tap the pulse, intone the pattern.

2. Intone the pulse, tap the pattern.

3. Tap the pulse with the right hand, the pattern with the left hand.

4. Reverse the function of the hands in (3)

5. Conduct the meter while intoning the pattern.

Exercise IV. Rhythmic Patterns in Various Meters

The examples given below provide practice in using rhythmic patterns in various meters. Note that the bar line is basically a convenience for the eye—it is not a stopping point or a breathing place. Each example should be performed so that it has a forward flow and musical continuity. Each bar must be thought of as only a small unit within the larger rhythmic units of phrase and period. (A *phrase* is a unit of musical form, usually from three to five measures in length. It is not to be confused with articulation—the use of slurs and staccato marks to indicate how a melody is to be performed.)

Glance through each example before performing it. Set the pulse and feel the meter before starting. Perform the examples as follows:

1. Intone the rhythmic pattern while clapping the pulse. Emphasize the first beat of each measure.

2. Clap or tap the rhythmic pattern while counting the pulses aloud.

3. Conduct the meter while intoning the pattern.

4. Perform each example at various tempos.

♩ = one pulse, o = two pulses, o· = three pulses

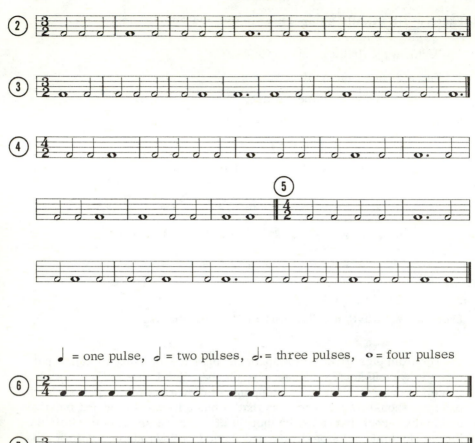

♩ = one pulse,   𝅝 = two pulses,   𝅗𝅥. = three pulses,   o = four pulses

♪ = one pulse,   ♩ = two pulses,   ♩. = three pulses

Exercise V. Ear Training

Invent simple rhythmic patterns, in various meters, similar to those in Exercise IV. Each pattern should be from four to seven measures in length. Dictate your pattern to the rest of the class by performing it several times. The pulse value must be announced ("the quarter note is the beat"). The class is to repeat the pattern, determine the meter by conducting, and, finally, write the pattern.

Exercise VI. Two-part Rhythmic Drills

Perform the examples given below as follows:

1. Half the class should perform the upper part, while the other half performs the lower part. Reverse parts.

2. The patterns may also be performed by tapping the upper part with one hand, the lower with the other hand.

Note that examples 5, 7, and 10 are canons. Imitation may begin at any distance as shown in the examples where the second voice waits one measure, one pulse, and two measures, respectively.

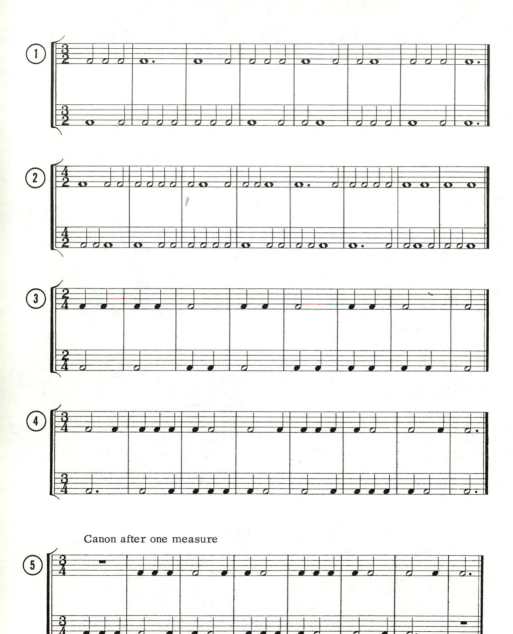

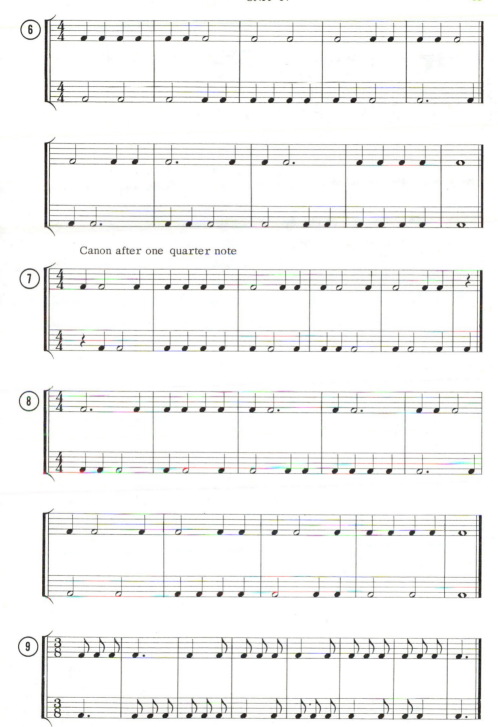

Canon after one quarter note

Canon after two measures

Exercise VII. Writing and Performing Original Canons

Each student should write an original rhythmic canon, put it on the blackboard, and then have it performed by the rest of the class. (In writing a canon be sure that there is rhythmic variety from measure to measure so that the contrast between voices can be heard.) The canons may be written for two, three, or four parts.

Exercise VIII. Melodies That Begin on a Tone Other Than the Tonic

Obviously not all melodies begin and end on the tonic of a key. Beginning on a tone other than the tonic is relatively common, but ending on a tone other than the tonic is comparatively rare. In order to determine the relationship of the starting tone to the tonic you must first find the tonic. Check the key signature and the ending tone, which is most probably the tonic of the key. Find the scale-degree number of the starting tone, relate it to the tonic, and perform the melody. Always retain the feeling of the tonic. In the first melody the key signature and the final tone show the melody to be in the key of C major. Start on C and sing the scale tones from 1 up to 5 and from 5 down to 1. Do the same from 8 down to 5 and back up to 8. Retain the feeling of the tonality of C major, thinking of the first tone as scale 7 which then moves up to scale 8, or 1.

Perform the melodies as follows:

Determine the key, then, while conducting the meter, sing the melody using (a) scale numbers, (b) conventional syllables, and (c) a neutral syllable.

Exercise IX. Ear Training

Invent simple melodic patterns which begin on various degrees of the scale. Be sure that each pattern ends on the tonic of the scale. Use stepwise motion and some leaps by thirds.

Dictate your pattern to the rest of the class by performing it several times. The name of the tonic tone must be announced. The class should sing back the pattern while conducting the meter. After identifying the first tone and its relation to the tonic tone the class should write the pattern.

Exercise X. The Movable "C" Clef

The C clef (𝄡) provides a convenient means of keeping the notation of music within a staff. This clef locates middle C and may be placed on any line of the staff. The *alto clef*, with middle C on the third line of the staff (𝄡 ⊙), and the *tenor clef*, with middle C on the

fourth line of the staff (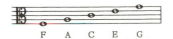), are in current use. The C clef is
also placed on the bottom line (soprano clef), the second line (mezzo-soprano clef), or the top line (baritone clef).

The exercise below presents studies using the alto clef. In reading this clef, do not attempt to transpose or to relate it to other clefs. Use the lines as guides, thinking of the pitch names of each:

Focus on the middle line (middle C) and concentrate on the spaces which surround that note (B and D). Similarly, concentrate on the spaces adjacent to the other lines of the staff.

Sing the studies in various tempos: (a) Name the pitches as they are sung. (b) Use conventional syllables. (c) Use scale-degree numbers. (d) Use a neutral syllable.

Exercise XI. Dictation Using the Alto Clef

Each student should write short phrases using the alto clef, and then play or sing each phrase several times. After the key is announced, the class should write the phrase using the alto clef.

UNIT V

Simple Subdivisions of the Beat;
Melodies Beginning on Upbeats;
Perfect Fourths and Fifths in the Major Scale;
the Major Triad; Chorale Melodies

In previous units two or more pulse notes were added together to make note values that were two, three, or four times as long as the pulse note. The process is reversed when the amount of time taken by one pulse note is divided into two or more parts. Such subdivision must be felt as an elaboration on the pulse, not as a mathematical abstraction.

The simplest kind of subdivision occurs when the pulse is divided into two equal parts.

Exercise I. Simple Subdivisions of the Pulse

1. While conducting in duple meter, sing, on a neutral syllable, two tones to each beat. Be sure that the tones are exactly even in length. The first tone of each measure should have a slight accent.

2. Sing even subdivisions of each beat while conducting triple meter.

3. Sing even subdivisions of each beat while conducting quadruple meter.

The notation of such subdivisions depends on the type of note which is chosen as pulse note:

Quadruple meter: ♫♫♫♫ ♩♩♩♩♩♩♩♩ ♫ ♫ ♫ ♫

Pulse: $\frac{4}{4}$ ♩ ♩ ♩ ♩ $\frac{4}{2}$ ♩ ♩ ♩ ♩ $\frac{4}{8}$ ♪ ♪ ♪ ♪

4. In duple meter, conduct the meter while singing alternate measures of pulse and subdivision: $\frac{2}{4}$ ‖: ♩ ♩ | ♫ ♫ :‖. Do this at least four times.

5. Conduct the meter while singing alternate pulse and subdivision:

$\frac{2}{4}$ ‖: ♩ ♫ :‖: ♫ ♩ :‖

6. In triple meter, conduct the meter while singing alternate measures of pulse notes and subdivisions: $\frac{3}{4}$ ‖: ♩ ♩ ♩ | ♫ ♫ ♫ :‖

7. Conduct triple meter while singing various arrangements of pulse notes and subdivisions:

8. Conduct quadruple meter while singing alternate measures of pulse notes and subdivisions:

$\frac{4}{4}$ ‖: ♩ ♩ ♩ ♩ | ♫ ♫ ♫ ♫ :‖

9. Conduct quadruple meter while singing various arrangements of pulse notes and subdivisions:

The various arrangements of pulse notes and subdivisions, as shown below, can be arranged into a list showing all the possible patterns using simple subdivisions of the beat in duple, triple, and quadruple meter. *Learn to recognize these measures as basic units rather than as a series of single notes.*

Patterns in duple meter:

      (1)   (2)   (3)   (4)

$\frac{2}{4}$ ♩ ♩ | ♫ ♫ | ♫ ♩ | ♩ ♫ | ♫ ♫ |

Patterns in triple meter:

(1)   (2)   (3)   (4)   (5)   (6)   (7)   (8)

$\frac{3}{4}$ ♩ ♩ ♩ | ♩ ♩ ♫ | ♩ ♫ ♩ | ♫ ♩ ♩ | ♫ ♫ ♩ | ♫ ♫ ♩ | ♫ ♩ ♫ | ♫ ♫ ♫ |

Patterns in quadruple meter:

Exercise II. Drills on Basic Subdivision Patterns

1. Sing or clap each of the measures given above. While singing, conduct the meter. While clapping, tap the pulse lightly with one foot. Perform each measure several times before moving on to the next measure.

2. Perform patterns made up of two or more measures—for example, in duple meter, units 1 and 3.

3. Each student chooses two, three, or four units within a meter to make a two-, three-, or four-measure rhythmic pattern. (It is permissible to repeat a measure in a four-measure pattern.) Each "composer" performs his pattern several times. The class repeats the pattern, identifies the units by referring to the list, and writes the pattern.

Exercise III. Rhythmic Phrases Emphasizing Subdivisions of the Beat

Perform the following patterns in various tempos. Glance through each pattern, noting where the pulse occurs.

1. Conduct the meter while intoning the pattern.

2. Tap the pulse with the left hand, the rhythmic pattern with the right hand. Repeat, reversing the duties of the hands.

3. Clap the pattern while counting aloud.

Pulse: | | | | | | etc.

Pulse: | | | | | etc.

Pulse: | | | | etc.

Pulse: | | | | | | etc.

Pulse: | | | | | | | etc.

Pulse: | | | | | |etc.

Pulse: | | | | | | | | etc.

Exercise IV. Conducting Music That Begins on an Upbeat

Not all music begins on the first beat of a measure. Many times a light beat precedes the heavy beat, as in poetry: "To bé or nót to bé." Music that begins on any beat other than the measure accent is said to begin on an upbeat, or *anacrusis*.

1. Practice conducting in meters of 2, 3, and 4. Begin on any beat other than the first beat. Give a light preparatory stroke preceding the upbeat.

2. Sing and conduct "The Star Spangled Banner," "Annie Laurie," "The First Nowell," "Clementine," and "Flow Gently, Sweet Afton." First find the meter of each song. Next find the measure accent and then the upbeat with which the music begins.

3. Conduct upbeats, changing hands on alternate measures:

Beat: 4   1   2   3,   4   1   2   3,   4   1   2   3,   etc.
         L.H.   R.H.   L.H.
                                                              etc.

If a recording of the first movement of Brahm's Fourth Symphony is available it can be used with the above example.

4. Find other musical examples that begin on upbeats—in folksongs, piano music, or symphonic music—and conduct them while singing or listening.

Exercise V. Rhythmic Patterns Based on Upbeats

1. Conduct the meter of each example while your eyes scan the pattern. Think the pulse from the beginning of a complete measure, but do not start to conduct until the pattern begins. (In the first pattern, for example, think, or say, "one-two-three," beginning the performance on "three.")

2. Intone the pattern while conducting the meter.

3. Tap the pattern while counting the beats aloud.

4. Tap the pattern with the right hand, the pulse with the left hand. Repeat, reversing the duties of the hands.

Upbeats often have a feeling of "lift" as they move toward the downbeats. The arrows above the following rhythmic patterns suggest where such a lift is felt. There can be a slight crescendo from upbeat to downbeat.

Note that an upbeat pattern usually recurs every measure or every other measure.

Exercise VI. Melodies Using Perfect Fourths and Fifths

Many melodies begin on the fifth degree of the scale and leap up or down to the tonic, or first degree. Such melodies often start on upbeats, as in the "Marseillaise" and "Flow Gently, Sweet Afton." The interval from the fifth scale degree *up* to the eighth scale degree is a *perfect fourth:* . From the fifth scale degree *down* to the tonic is a *perfect fifth:* . Accustom your eyes to measure distances on the staff so that recognizing the size of an interval becomes automatic. Note that in the perfect fourth one note is on a space, the other on a line. In the perfect fifth both notes are on spaces or lines.

1. Before attempting to sing the whole melody, fix the sound of the tonic securely in your mind. Sing the tonic and fifth scale degree above and below the tonic. Remember the sound of the perfect fourth and the perfect fifth and the "feel" of these intervals in the voice. If you have difficulty in singing the intervals of the perfect fifth, mentally insert the scale tones that fall between the two tones: 5-(6-7)-8; 8-(7-6)-5; 1-(2-3-4)-5; 5-(4-3-2)-1.

2. Conduct the meters of the following melodies and sing them, using (a) scale-degree numbers, (b) letter names, (c) conventional syllables, and (d) a neutral syllable.

3rd of I, V chord
must be high

1♩ = 24

Exercise VII. Drills on Perfect Fourths and Fifths

1. Sing perfect fourths *above* given piano tones. (Think of scale degrees 5-8.)

2. Sing perfect fourths *below* given piano tones. (Think of scale degrees 8-5.)

3. Sing perfect fifths *above* given piano tones. (Think of scale degrees 1-5.)

4. Sing perfect fifths *below* given piano tones. (Think of scale degrees 5-1.)

The above exercises can be sung in a rhythmic pattern: a tone is given on the first pulse; the class matches that tone on the second pulse; the class sings the specified interval on the third pulse and holds that tone through the fourth pulse.

Singing a perfect fourth <u>above</u> a given tone

5. Sing short "chains" of intervals, such as:

    (a) Perfect fifth up, minor third down.

    (b) Perfect fourth up, minor second down.

    (c) Perfect fourth up, perfect fifth down.

        Etc.

6. Identify perfect fourths and perfect fifths when played on the piano harmonically and melodically.

Exercise VIII. Ear Training

Invent short major scale melodies similar to those in Exercise VI. Each melody should contain perfect fourths or perfect fifths that are based on scale degrees 1-5 or 5-8.

1. Each individual plays or sings his melody three times, first announcing the key.

2. After the third hearing the class sings the melody once or twice.

3. The class members write the melody and check their versions against the correct version written on the blackboard by the student who composed the melody.

Exercise IX. Singing Perfect Fourths and Placing Them
in Key Relationships

Perfect fourths occur in the ascending major scale from 1 to 4, 2 to 5, 3 to 6, 5 to 8, 6 to 2, and 7 to 3:

The first tone in each of the following is to be played on the piano.

1. Sing the given tone and a perfect fourth above it. Call the tones 1-4 of a major scale and sing down the scale: 1-4-3-2-1.

2. Sing a perfect fourth, ascending. Call the tones 2-5 of a major scale and sing down the scale 2-5-4-3-2-1.

3. Sing a perfect fourth, descending. Call the tones 6-3 of a major scale and sing 6-3-5-4-3-2-1.

4. Sing a perfect fourth, descending. Call the tones 8-5 and sing 8-5-6-7-8.

5. Sing a perfect fourth, descending. Call the tones 2-6 and sing 2-6-7-5-8.

6. Sing a perfect fourth, ascending. Call the tones 7-3 and sing 7-3-2-1.

7. Sing all perfect fourths, in a major scale ascending, starting on the tonic. Choose a starting tone which is low. The pattern will be: 1-4, 2-5, 3-6, 5-8, 6-2, 7-3-1.

8. Sing all the perfect fourths in a descending major scale. Choose a starting tone which is high. The pattern will be: 8-5, 6-3, 5-2, 4-1, 3-7, 2-6-1.

Exercise X. Singing Perfect Fifths and Placing Them
in Key Relationships

Perfect fifths occur in the major scale ascending from 1 to 5, 2 to 6, 3 to 7, 4 to 8, 5 to 2, 6 to 3:

The first tone in each of the following is to be played on the piano.

1. Sing the given tone and a perfect fifth above it. Call the tones 1-5 of a major scale and sing down the scale: 1-5-4-3-2-1.

2. Sing a perfect fifth, ascending. Call the tones 2-6 of a major scale and sing 2-6-5-4-3-2-1.

3. Sing a perfect fifth, ascending. Call the tones 3-7 of a major scale and sing 3-7-8-5-8.

4. Sing a perfect fifth, descending. Call the tones 8-4 of a major scale and sing 8-4-5-4-3-2-1.

5. Sing a perfect fifth, ascending. Call the tones 5-2 of a major scale and sing 5-2-5-6-7-8.

6. Sing a perfect fifth, ascending. Call the tones 6-3 of a major scale and sing 6-3-2-1-5-6-7-8.

7. Sing all the perfect fifths in an ascending major scale. Choose a starting tone which is low. The pattern will be: 1-5, 2-6, 3-7, 4-8, 5-2, 6-3-1.

8. Sing all the perfect fifths in a descending major scale. Choose a starting tone which is high. The pattern will be: 8-4, 7-3, 6-2, 5-1, 3-6, 2-5-1.

Exercise XI. Intervals Within the Major Triad

A *triad* is a chord consisting of three tones. In traditional harmony a triad is built in a series of thirds above the generating tone, or *root*. The first, third, and fifth tones of a major scale combine to form a *major triad*.

1. Start on a given tone. Sing the chord numbers of a major triad based on that tone:

   (a) 1-3-5-3-1

   (b) 1-3-5-8-5-3-1

   (c) 1-5-3-5-8-5-1

   (d) 1-5-8-5-1-8-1

   (e) 1-5-8-5-8-3̄-8-5-3̄-8

   (f) 1-3-5-3-5-8-3-8-1

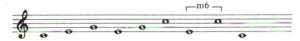

   (g) 1-5-8-3-8-5-3̄-5-8

2. The interval from 1 to 8, and any duplication of a tone at its next higher or lower pitch, is an octave. Practice singing octaves above and below all tones of a triad—within the possibilities of your voice.

3. The interval from 5 up to 3, as in (e) above, is a major sixth. Practice singing this interval in the major triad. Play the root on the piano, then sing the pattern 1-5-3̄: ex. [musical example] . Do the above on various pitches.

4. The interval from 3 up to 8, as in (f) above, is a minor sixth. Practice singing this interval in the major triad. Play the root on the piano; then sing the pattern 1-3-8: ex. [musical example] . Do the above on various pitches.

5. Sing major triads above a series of given tones on the piano as in the example below. Call each given tone the "one" or root of the triad.

6. A series of given tones is to be thought of as the "5s," or fifths, of major triads. Sing down the triad from the given pitch, as in the example:

SUMMARY OF SKIPS WITHIN THE MAJOR TRIAD

(a) Major third (1 up to 3, 3 down to 1)
(b) Minor third (3 up to 5, 5 down to 3)
(c) Perfect fifth (1 up to 5, 5 down to 1)
(d) Perfect fourth (5 up to 8, 8 down to 5)
(e) Perfect octave (1 to 8, 3 to 3, 5 to 5)
(f) Major sixth (5 up to 3, 3 down to 5)
(g) Minor sixth (3 up to 8, 8 down to 3)

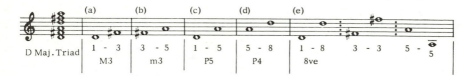

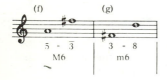

Exercise XII. Melodic Patterns Based on the Major Triad

Each study given below is based on the major triad built on the tonic tone of the key. Learn to recognize the shape of each triad so that it can be thought of as a unit rather than as a series of individual notes.

1. Think the numbers 1, 3, 5 while scanning each melody to establish the position of each note in the triad. Sing each melody on chord numbers (1-3-5).

2. Sing the melodies at various speeds. Use (a) conventional syllables, (b) a neutral syllable, and (c) pitch names.

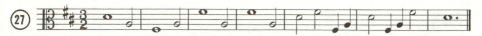

Exercise XIII. Ear Training

Each student should make up a melody, based on a major triad, similar to the melodies of Exercise XII, and then perform each melody several times for the class, announcing first the meter and key. The class sings the melody on chord numbers (1-3-5) and then writes it.

Exercise XIV. Chorale Melodies

Chorales are hymn tunes of the Lutheran church. Early versions of the tunes are quite free, metrically and rhythmically. By 1700 the chorales were metric and had a regular rhythm that followed the syllables of the texts. The fermatas (⌢) over certain tones indicate the ends of phrases. If the phrase is a long one, a breath should be taken at the fermata. In some cases, taking a breath will mean that the note will have to be lengthened.

The chorales given below contain leaps of thirds and leaps within the tonic triad. Notice that one chorale melody appears in three different versions.

Before singing the chorale:

1. Determine the key and locate the tonic.

2. Scan the melody, and note the fermatas that indicate phrase endings.

3. Make a note of the leaps, particularly those within the tonic triad.

4. Set the pulse before singing.

Sing the chorales on (a) scale-degree numbers, (b) conventional syllables, and (c) a neutral syllable.

UNIT VI

Melodies Based on Primary Harmonies; the Dominant Seventh; Rhythmic Canons; Rests; Excerpts from Music Literature

One of the fundamental unifying features in music, from 1600 to the present, has been the concept of harmonic relationships. Within a key all chords tend to move, in various progressions, toward the triad built on the tonic, or keynote, of the scale. A chord may be built on any tone of a scale. The *primary chords* are those built on the primary tones of a scale: the tonic (I) on the first degree; the dominant (V) on the fifth degree; and the sub-dominant (IV) on the fourth degree. In the major scale these three chords are major triads.

Exercise I. Drills on the Primary Chords in the Major Scale

1. Sing an ascending major scale, starting on D.

2. Sing the first, fourth, and fifth scale degrees of the key of D.

3. Sing major triads up from these tones. Use triad numbers (root-third-fifth), scale-degree numbers, conventional syllables, and a neutral syllable.

4. Do the above (3) in the keys of G, C, E♭, B♭ and A. If the tones go too high sing the IV and the V below the tonic:

Exercise II. Melodies Based on Primary Triads

Melodies frequently reflect the harmonic organization of a work by spelling out all the notes of the prevailing harmony or by using some of the notes of a chord in a significant manner. Learn to group tones into

67

harmonic patterns, whether in sight singing or in ear training. Such reading is analogous to reading a language by words and phrases rather than letter by letter.

1. Scan the following melodies. Think the proper numeral (I, IV, V) that best fits the chords outlined in the melody. Notice that the harmonies change at a fairly regular rate of speed—every measure, every other measure, every other beat, etc. (The rate of speed of harmonic change is called *harmonic rhythm*.)

2. Sing the melodies (a) on scale-degree numbers, (b) on pitch names, (c) on conventional syllables, and (d) on a neutral syllable.

Exercise III. Intervals Within the Dominant Seventh

The dominant harmony (V) is frequently made a four-tone chord by the addition of a tone which lies a minor third above the top tone of the dominant triad:  . Such a chord is called a *dominant*

seventh (V7). The scale-degree numbers in the V_7 are: 5-7-2-4.

1. Sing, in the keys of G, B♭, and F the following scale-degree patterns:

    (a) 8-5-8-7-8-2-3-4-2-7-5-7-8

    Key of C

    (b) 8-5-7-2-4-2-7-5-8

    Key of C

    (c) 5-7-2-4-2-7-5

    Key of C

    (d) Sing the pitches of (c) using the chord numbers of the V_7:
        R-3-5-7-5-3-R   (R= root)

2. Sing dominant sevenths starting on various pitches.

3. In the key of G sing these patterns in the V_7:

    (a) R-3-5-7-3-5-R

    (b) R-3-5-7-R-7-5-3

    (c) R-5-3-7-3-5-7-R

4. The interval between the third and the seventh of the V_7 is called a
    diminished fifth:  . It occurs between scale degrees 7
    and 4 and usually moves to a tone of the tonic chord. Starting on
    various tonics sing these scale-degree patterns:

    (a) 8-7-4-3

    (b) 3-4-7-8

5. When the diminished fifth is *inverted* (turned upside down) it be-

comes an augmented fourth: . The diminished

fifth and the augmented fourth are equal in size. Each spans the distance of three whole steps which gives them their common name,
tritone. Starting on various tonics sing these scale-degree patterns:

   (a) 8-5-4-7-8

   (b) 8-7-4-3-5-8

   (c) 8-7-4-5-4-3

Key of C

6. The interval between the root and the seventh of the V₇ (scale de-

grees 5 up to 4) is called a *minor seventh:*  .   The

seventh is usually followed by another tone of the V₇, or moves on
to the third of the scale:

Starting on various pitches sing these tones of a dominant seventh:

   (a) R-3-5-7

   (b) R-5-7

   (c) R-7-R

7. Distinguish between minor sevenths and tritones played harmonically and melodically on the piano.

SUMMARY OF SKIPS WITHIN THE DOMINANT SEVENTH

The dominant seventh contains all the intervals of the major triad
plus the following:

(a) Minor seventh (R up to 7, 7 down to R)
(b) Major second (R down to 7, 7 up to R)
(c) Diminished fifth (3 up to 7, 7 down to 3)
(d) Augmented fourth (3 down to 7, 7 up to 3)

      Min.7   Maj.2   Dim.5   Aug.4

Exercise IV. Melodies Built on the Primary Triads and the Dominant Seventh

Scan each of the following melodies before attempting to sing them. Think the primary chords of the key of each melody. Look for these chord formations as well as for repeated melodic and rhythmic patterns. When singing the melodies do not stop. If there is a troublesome passage isolate it, practice it until it can be sung without error, and then attempt the whole melody again. Be sure to set the pulse before singing.

While conducting the meter, sing the following melodies (a) on scale-degree numbers, (b) on conventional syllables, and (c) on a neutral syllable.

Italian folk song

German folk song

Scottish dance tune

American dance tune

American dance tune

Scottish (early version)

German folk song

Purcell

Exercise V. Ear Training

Each student is to invent a melodic line which contains skips within the I, IV, V, and V$_7$ chords. The rhythmic pattern of the melody should use simple subdivisions of the beat. Each student-composer should perform his melody several times, announcing the key and meter. After several hearings the class should sing the melody and then write it, checking against the original which can be sung on pitch names or written on the blackboard.

Exercise VI. Review of Perfect Fourths and Perfect Fifths

1. One student starts by singing a tone in the low register. The next student sings that tone and the tone which lies a perfect fifth higher. The third student repeats the last tone and sings a tone which is a perfect fourth lower. Continue this pattern of up a fifth, down a fourth, around the class.

2. Repeat the procedure of (1), starting in a high register, and sing a pattern of down a perfect fifth, up a perfect fourth.

3. Start on a given tone and perform the patterns in unison.

Exercise VII. Two-part Rhythmic Studies

1. Perform the following material with half the class intoning the upper part while the other half taps the lower part. Reverse parts. Be sure to set the pulse before starting.

2. Tap both parts simultaneously (right and left hands).

3. Intone the lower part while clapping the upper.

4. Intone the upper part while clapping the lower.

    Perform each exercise several times at different tempos.

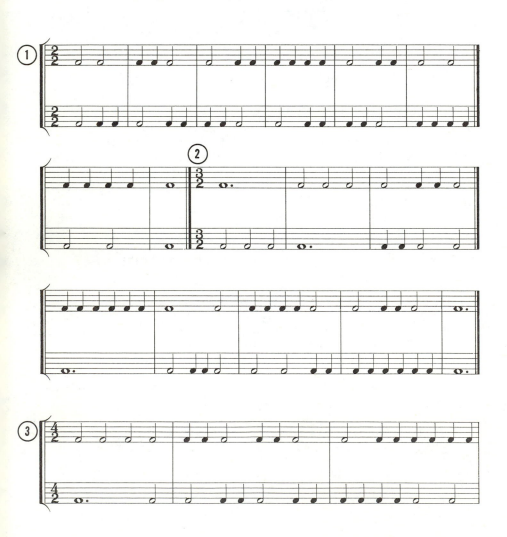

Rhythmic canon after one measure

The lower voice has a rhythmic ostinato.

Exercise VIII. Original Two-part Rhythmic Canons

Write several two-part rhythmic canons similar to No. 6, above, using simple subdivisions of the pulse. Perform as duets. A good canon has rhythmic variety so that one voice has movement while the other holds.

Exercise IX. Improvised Canons

In a meter of four counts, one student, at the piano, invents a one-measure rhythmic pattern. The class claps this pattern while the leader plays a second improvised measure. (The class must listen for its next measure while performing its first measure.) Continue for four to eight measures.

Repeat with new leaders. Use various meters, always sounding the pulse for one full measure before beginning.

Exercise X. Rests

In this exercise rests of various kinds are introduced:

$$\mathbf{■.} = \mathbf{o.}, \quad \mathbf{■} = \mathbf{o}, \quad \mathbf{■.} = \mathbf{d.}, \quad \mathbf{■} = \mathbf{d}, \quad \mathbf{\S} = \mathbf{d}, \quad \mathbf{\gamma} = \mathbf{\flat}, \quad \mathbf{\gamma} = \mathbf{\flat}, \quad \mathbf{\gamma} = \mathbf{\flat}.$$

Occasionally a whole rest is used to indicate a one-measure rest, regardless of the meter. In instrumental music a whole rest with a number above it or below it indicates a specific number of measures of rest:

Perform the exercises below at various tempos:

1. Intone the rhythm while clapping the pulse.

2. Conduct the meter while intoning the rhythm.

3. Tap the pulse with the right hand, the rhythm with the left hand. Reverse this procedure.

Using one-beat rests

Using one-, two-, three-, and four-beat rests

Using rests which subdivide the beat

Pulse: | | | | | | | | etc.

Exercise XI. Ear Training

Invent a short rhythmic pattern, two to four measures in length, which uses simple subdivided beats and rests. Perform your pattern several times. The class should then write the pattern.

Exercise XII. Two-voiced Rhythmic Patterns

Perform the two-part material below:

1. with half the class speaking the upper part while the other half claps the lower part.

2. as a duet for two soloists.

3. by tapping the upper part with the right hand and the lower part with the left hand.

Canon after two measures

④

⑤

Canon in retrograde*

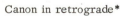

⑥

*Retrograde motion is backward motion. Here the lower voice is an imitation
of the upper voice—starting with the last note of the upper voice and moving
backwards.

Exercise XIII. Excerpts from Music Literature

The following compositions utilize all the elements of Unit VI—chordal melodic lines, rests, two-part rhythmic patterns and canons for three or more voices. The canons (Nos. 2 and 3) should be sung first in unison, and then with the voices entering every two measures. In No. 3 all voices end on the first beat of the measure, indicated by the fermata. No. 4 may be sung as S-A-B, S-T-B, or S-S-A (with the alto singing the bass line an octave higher than written). Sing each composition on (a) scale-degree numbers, (b) conventional syllables, and (c) a neutral syllable.

Bach

Four-voice canon   Anonymous

Six-part canon   Haydn

*On a signal all voices will end on the next note that has a fermata over it.

Mozart

Fine

D.C. al Fine

UNIT VII

Dotted Notes and Tied Notes; the Minor Triad;
the Diminished Triad; Leaps in All Diatonic Triads;
Further Drills on Perfect Fourths
and Perfect Fifths; Excerpts from Music Literature

The rhythmic studies given below emphasize the use of dotted notes and tied notes. Such notes should always be held for their full value. When tapping patterns your fingers should maintain contact, for the duration of each note, with the object being tapped (arm, book, etc.).

In performing patterns that use dotted notes and tied notes it is imperative to feel where the pulse lies. For rhythmic accuracy the dot after a note should be thought of as a replacement for a note half as long as the note itself: ♩. = ♩‿♪ = ♩+♪

Exercise I. Rhythmic Patterns Containing Dotted Notes and Tied Notes

Perform the drills in the following manner:

1. Intone the rhythmic pattern while conducting the meter.

2. Tap the pattern with one hand while tapping the pulse with the other. Repeat the pattern, reversing the duties of each hand.

3. Tap the pulse with one foot, the half pulse with the left hand, and the pattern with the right hand. Repeat the pattern reversing the duties of the hands. It is sometimes a bit easier to set the pulse and the half pulse for a few measures before beginning the pattern.

(Ex. No.1 below)

Some of the drills are quite difficult to perform and will require a certain amount of practice before good body co-ordination is acquired.

Exercise II. Ear Training

Each student is to invent a rhythmic pattern, four to six measures in length, which utilizes dotted notes and tied notes. These patterns should be dictated to the rest of the class, with the pulse note announced and sounded several times. After several hearings of the pattern the class is to repeat the pattern, determine the meter, and write the pattern.

Exercise III. Drills on the Minor Triad in a Major Key

The minor triad contains the same intervals as does the major triad, but in a different order—a minor third plus a major third.

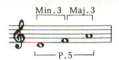

1. Play a tone. Sing the given tone and the tone a minor third above it. (Think scale degrees 6-8, 2-4, 3-5.) Repeat on various pitches.

2. Play a tone. Sing the given tone and the tone a major third above it. (Think scale degrees 1-3, 4-6, 5-7.) Repeat on various pitches.

3. Start with a tone. Sing a major third plus a minor third above the given tone. (Think scale degrees 6-8-3, 2-4-6, 3-5-7.) Repeat on various pitches.

4. Start on a tone. Sing the following series of tones of the minor triad based on the starting tone:

    (a) R (Root)-3-5-3-R

    (b) R-3-5-8-5-3-R

    (c) R-5-3-5-8-5-R

    (d) R-5-8-5-R-8-5-3-R

    Repeat the above, starting on other pitches.

5. On the first beat of a four-count measure, play a tone which will be the root of a minor triad. On successive beats, sing R-3-5. Use a different starting tone on the first beat of each measure:

6. Do as above, calling the first tone the fifth of the triad. Sing 5-3-R:

7. Do as above, calling the first tone the fifth of the triad. Sing 5-R-3:

8. Do as above, calling the first tone the third of a minor triad. Sing 3-R-5:

9. Do as above, calling the first tone the third of a minor triad. Sing 3-5-R:

Exercise IV. Minor Triads in the Major Scale

In the major scale, minor triads occur on the second scale degree (supertonic), the third scale degree (mediant), and the sixth scale degree (submediant).

Sing the following harmonic progressions following the pattern of the example. Repeat on several different tonics.

(a)   I-VI-I; I-II-I; I-III-I

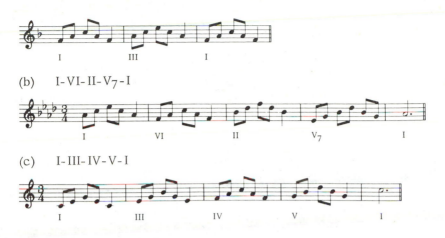

(b)   I-VI-II-V₇-I

(c)   I-III-IV-V-I

Exercise V. Melodies Based on the Tonic, Supertonic, Subdominant, and Dominant Chords

The most common minor triad in a major key is that which is built on the supertonic (II). The supertonic is often used as part of a cadence progression, preceding the dominant.

The melodies given below contain leaps within the I, II, IV, V and V_7 chords. Analyze the harmonic structure of each melody. Think, or mark, the chord numerals for the entire melody before attempting to sing it. Improvise simple accompaniments on the piano while singing the melodies. The examples show three basic piano accompaniment patterns which might be used with the first melody. (The symbol ⁒ means that the previous measure is to be repeated.)

(c)

1. Sing the melodies on conventional syllables, scale-degree numbers, and a neutral syllable.

2. Half the class should sing the melody while the other half sings the root of the harmony of the moment.

①

②

Exercise VI.   The Diminished Triad

In the key of D major sing the following pattern of scale degrees:

1   7   1   2   3   4   2   7   2   4   2   7   2   4

The chord on scale degrees 7-2-4 is a *diminished triad.* (It is identical with the three upper tones of a dominant seventh.) The only diminished triad in a major key is that which is built on the seventh degree of the scale, the *leading tone.* Other than octaves the diminished triad contains three intervals and their inversions:

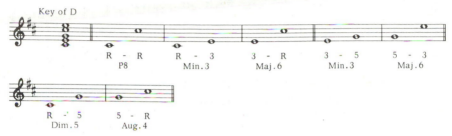

1. Play a tone which is to be the tonic (I) of a major scale. Sing the diminished triad of that scale in this manner:

Continue this pattern in strict rhythm, with a new tonic every second measure.

2. Play a tone which is to be the third of a major scale. Sing the diminished triad of that scale in this manner:

Continue this pattern, with a new third of a scale every second measure.

3. Sing the melodies below on syllables and on scale-degree numbers.

Exercise VII.   Melodies Based on All Diatonic Triads and the Dominant Seventh

Scan each melody before attempting to perform it. Analyze the harmonic structure and accustom your eyes to encompass units that take a whole measure or more. Harmonic units should be sung as units, not as a series of individual notes. When scanning the melody visualize how the rhythmic pattern relates to the basic pulse. Conduct the meter.

1. Sing each melody (a) on conventional syllables, (b) on scale-degree numbers, and (c) on a neutral syllable.

2. Half the class is to sing the melody while the other half sings the root of the harmony in each measure.

3. Improvise simple piano accompaniments, similar to those in Exercise VI.

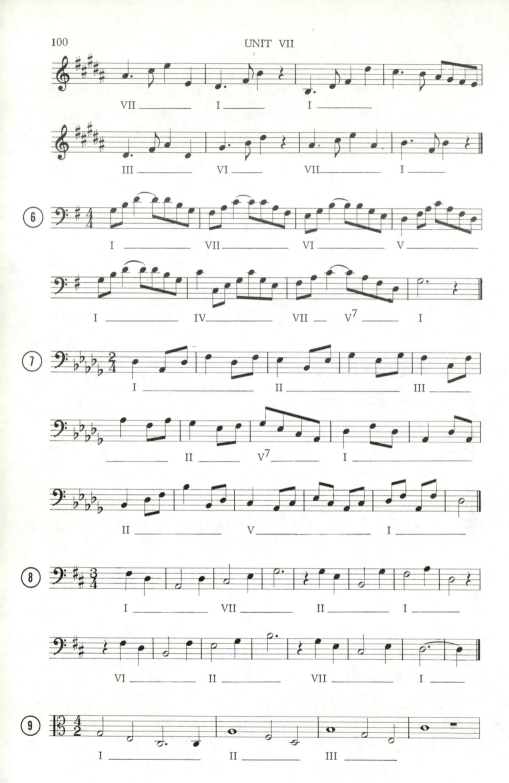

Exercise VIII. Ear Training

Write a melody which features leaps within the various triads in a major key. There should be some use of repetition, either exact or sequential, as in the melodies of Exercise VIII. Use not more than three different rhythmic patterns in one melody.

After announcing the key and the pulse note, perform your melody several times for the rest of the class, which then writes the melody from your dictation.

Exercise IX. Drills on Perfect Fourths and Perfect Fifths

The intervals of the perfect fourth and the perfect fifth usually represent the root and fifth of triads and are therefore so important that they must be sung with perfect intonation. Sing each of the following examples, at various speeds, on conventional syllables, on scale-degree numbers, and on a neutral syllable. (Each drill may be sung backward as well as forward.)

Exercise X. Excerpts from Music Literature

    The melodies in this exercise utilize most of the problems presented thus far. Before attempting performance, scan each melody, noting its distinctive pitch and rhythmic problems. Note repetitions and sequences, phrasing, melodic climax, etc. Establish both the feeling of the tonic tone of the key and the basic pulse before starting.

Innig (Andante molto sostenuto)   R. Franz

Campion

Mozart

Three-voice canon   H. Lawes

⑦

Great   Tom   is   cast,   and   Christ Church Bells ring

one,   two, three, four, five,   six,   and Tom comes   last.

Three-part canon   S. Webbe

⑧

Now   we are met let____ mirth a - bound,   Now we are met let

mirth a - bound.   And let the catch,   and let the catch,

and let the catch and toast____ go round,   And toast go

round,   and toast go round, let the catch and   toast   go   round.

Schubert

⑨

Note leap of a major ninth.

Three-part round   Purcell

*Major 9th

scale 5 - 6

*Think of scale degrees 5-6, with the 6
an octave higher than usual.

J. J. Fux

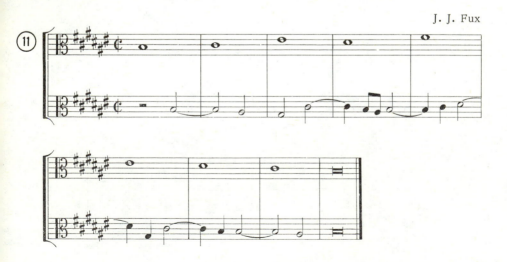

Padre Martini

Josquin des Prez

a   vir -   gi -   ne.

a   vir -   gi -   ne.

Four-part canon   Hayes

Here   lies   my   wife poor

let her lie, let her lie,   let her lie

pose,   she   finds   re-pose, re - pose at

I, and so do I,   and so do I, and so do   I,   so do

Coda*

* After the canon is performed several times, a signal is given in the last measure and each performer sings the coda keeping to the same line.

UNIT VIII

Forms of the Minor Scale;
Further Subdivisions of the Beat;
Excerpts from Music Literature

Exercise I. The Minor Scale

1. Sing and study the melody of the Shakespearean song, "How Should I Your True Love Know":

Notice:

(a) The tonic is G.

(b) The interval outlined in the first three tones, from the first to the third degree of the scale, is a minor third.

(c) The seventh tone of the scale (F♯) is raised to create an active push to the tonic in measure 2.

(d) The most important tones of the melody (G-B♭-D) outline the tonic triad of the scale. This triad is minor in quality. Most of the significant leaps in the melody occur between tones of the tonic triad.

110

The intervals of the minor third between the first and third tones of the scale and the major third between the third and fifth tones of the scale are important features of the various forms of the minor scale. (The chief characteristic of the minor scale is that its third tone is a minor third above the tonic. In old music texts the minor scale was identified as "the scale with the lesser [minor] third.")

2. Starting on D, sing the first five tones of the major scale, ascending, followed by the tonic triad, descending:

Contrast it with the minor form made by lowering the third degree by a half step:

3. Do the above, starting on various pitches.

4. Call B♭ the fifth tone of a major scale. Sing down to the tonic. Follow this by the tonic triad, ascending:

Contrast this with the minor form:

5. Sing the above patterns (4) from various starting pitches.

Exercise II. The Three Forms of the Minor Scale

There are three forms of the minor scale: the natural, the harmonic, and the melodic. All three forms use the same pattern for their first five notes:

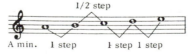

Note the minor second, or half step, between the second and third tones.

1. Starting on various pitches sing the minor scale pattern from 1 up to 5 and from 5 down to 1.

The three forms of the minor scale differ in the patterns used between the fifth and the eighth tones of the scales:

(a) Natural minor (Aeolian mode)—like a major scale from 6 to 6.

(b) Harmonic minor—distinguished by the half steps between 5-6, 7-8 and the augmented second (a step and a half) between 6 and 7:

(c) Melodic minor, which combines the fifth, sixth, seventh, and eighth degrees of a major scale, ascending; with the seventh, sixth and fifth degrees of the natural minor, descending:

2. Practice singing 5-6-7-8-7-6-5 in the three forms of the minor scale:

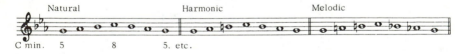

Repeat these patterns, starting on various pitches.

3. Decide on a tonic and a form of the minor scale, then sing from 5 up to 8 and from 8 down to 1. Do this with five or six different notes as tonics.

4. Sing the complete ascending and descending scale of each form of minor, starting on various tonics.

Exercise III. Drills on the Primary Chords in the Harmonic Minor Scale

The harmonic form of the minor scale has been the one most often used in music since 1650. The chord formations in that scale are, therefore, the most essential to know. In the harmonic scale the I and IV chords are minor, the V is major:

1. Sing an ascending harmonic minor scale, starting on D.

2. Sing the first, fourth, and fifth scale degrees of D, harmonic minor.

3. Sing the triads based on these tones. Use triad numbers (root-third-fifth), scale-degree numbers, conventional syllables, and a neutral syllable.

4. Do the above (3) in the keys of G, C, Eb, Bb, and A harmonic minors. If the tones go too high sing the IV and the V below the tonic:

Exercise IV. Melodic Studies in the Minor Scale

Scan the following studies to discover which form of minor scale is used. Notice where chordal patterns occur. Sing the melodies (a) on numbers, representing scale degrees, (b) on conventional syllables, (c) on a neutral syllable.

Conduct the meter as the study is being sung. Sing each study at various tempos.

Exercise V. Ear Training

Invent short melodic lines in various minor keys. Use mainly step-wise motion but include leaps within the primary chords in the harmonic minor. Perform your melody several times. After you announce the key, the rest of the class should write the melody from your dictation.

Exercise VI. Further Subdivisions of the Beat

The rhythmic material given below presents further subdivisions of the beat, using sixteenth- and thirty-second notes. Choose a slow or moderate tempo at first and increase the speed on subsequent practice. Try not to stop during the performance of each drill.

Mentally mark off the first note of each beat, in the first few drills. Learn to recognize the beginning of each beat without hesitation. Think of formations such as ♫♫♫ , ♪♫ , and ♫♫♫♪ as units, with an impetus moving from pulse to pulse. Look ahead! Be prepared for the rhythmic problems that must be faced in the following beats or measures. Your eyes should always be focused on what lies ahead rather than on what is being done.

Perform the patterns as follows:

1. Intone the pattern while conducting the meter.

2. Tap the pattern with the right hand, the pulse with the left hand.

3. Reverse hands.

Exercise VII. Ear Training

Each student is to invent a 4-6 measure rhythmic pattern similar to those in Exercise V. After announcing the pulse note perform your pattern several times. The class is to determine the meter, repeat the pattern, and then write the pattern from dictation.

Exercise VIII. Two-part Rhythmic Drills

Perform the two-part rhythmic drills given below in the following ways:

1. Half the class taps the upper part while the other half claps the lower part. Reverse the parts.

2. As a duet for two soloists.

3. Tap the upper part with the right hand and the lower part with the left hand. Reverse parts.

4. In doing (1) and (3), have a member of the class conduct the performance and make corrections.

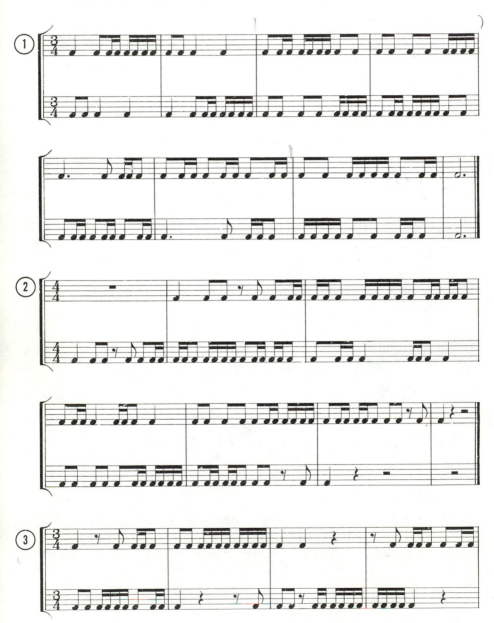

Exercise IX. Excerpts from Music Literature

Perform the following excerpts while conducting the meter. Scan each work before doing it, looking for harmonic formations and noticing the subdivisions of the pulse. Each composition should be sung (a) on scale-degree numbers, (b) on conventional syllables, (c) on a neutral syllable, and (d) with the text––where it is supplied.

Four-part round

Anonymous

1.   2.

① Thou poor bird, Mourn'st the tree, Where

3.   4.

sweet-ly thou did'st war-ble in thy wan - d'rings free.

Folk song

②

Scandanavian folk song

Rameau

Schubert

L. Couperin

12

Three-part canon

Byrd

13

Schubert

14

Mozart

Presto

Mozart

Allegretto   Mozart

Andante   Mozart

Andante   Handel

Ev - 'ry val - ley,   ev - 'ry val - ley ___ shall be ex-alt - ed,

shall be _____ ex-alt   -   -

-        -   -   -   ed.

Massig   Weber

UNIT IX

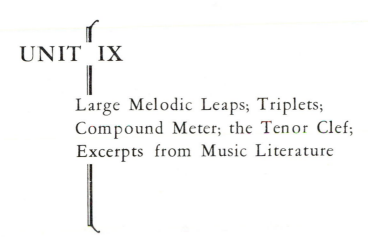

Large Melodic Leaps; Triplets;
Compound Meter; the Tenor Clef;
Excerpts from Music Literature

Large melodic leaps are seldom found in music written before 1600, but since that time they have been used in increasing numbers.

The intervals of sixths, sevenths, and ninths frequently create sight-singing difficulties. In tonal music it is best to think of these intervals in relation to their scale functions; but even at the beginning it is good practice to train the ear to hear the difference between the major seventh (scale 1 up to 7) and the minor seventh (scale 2 up to 8) and the major sixth (1 up to 6 in the major scale) and the minor sixth (3 up to 8 in the major scale).

Exercise I. Large Melodic Leaps

Sing the following exercises, using scale numbers and conventional syllables. Always retain the feeling for the tonic of the scale.

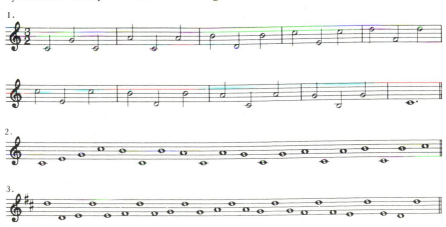

Often, in melodies containing many large leaps, there is a relation between successive high tones or low tones. In (1), p. 133, the successive high tones move by step from G up to D and back again. In (2), the high tones move down by step from the eighth to the fifth tones of the scale and then back, by step to the eighth tone. In (3) the top tone is always the tonic; the lower tones move from the first to the sixth tones of the scale and then back to 1.

A study of the following melody by Handel shows a stepwise relation between the high pitches from measure 9 to the end. There is also a stepwise relation between the low pitches in the same measures.

(a)   Handel

An analysis of the melody, from the ninth measure to the end, shows, in effect, a two-part texture (b). This is typical of many long melodic lines from the Baroque period.

(b)

Exercise II. Singing Melodic Outlines

1. The melody given below is a skeletonized version of the last part of the melody by Handel. Sing it on scale-degree numbers and syllables.

2. Sing the Handel melody in its original form. Use scale-degree numbers and syllables.

Exercise III. Melodies Containing Large Leaps

Sing the melodic studies given below, using scale numbers, conventional syllables, and a neutral syllable. Note the relationships between the high pitches and between the low pitches. Sing each study at different tempos, conducting while singing. Where difficult passages occur, isolate the troublesome spots and practice them before attempting the whole melody again.

Exercise IV. Ear Training

1. Write a melody containing several leaps of sixths and sevenths. Be sure that between the high pitches, as well as the low pitches, there is a stepwise or common tone relationship. Each melody should be played or sung several times, after which the class should sing back the melody. The key should be announced and the melody then written from dictation.

2. Find and bring in to class instrumental or vocal melodies containing large leaps (the works of Bach and Handel are good sources). These melodies may be dictated or written on the blackboard and used for further sight-singing practice.

3. Identify various major and minor sixths and major and minor sevenths when played by two instruments or on the piano.

Exercise V. Concentrated Drills on Large Leaps

1. Practice singing major and minor sixths and major and minor sevenths in the following manner:

(a) On the first beat of a four-count measure, a pitch is played on the piano. On the second beat, the class matches that pitch, and on the third and fourth beats, sings the specified interval. A new pitch is then played and the pattern is repeated:

This drill should be done rhythmically, without loss of a beat. If errors are made, the same pitch should be played in the next measure and so on, until the correct pattern is sung.

(b) Perform the above drill by having each student, in turn, sing one pattern.

2. The drills given below utilize large leaps almost exclusively. Sing each drill at various speeds. Always keep in mind the sense of tonic and dominant pitches. Use conventional syllables, a neutral syllable, scale-degree numbers, and, at a slow tempo, pitch names.

Exercise VI. The Triplet

The normal subdivision of a beat, or part of a beat, is in two or four parts. However, any beat, or part of a beat, may also be divided into three equal parts. Such a subdivision is called a *triplet*. Each of the rhythmic drills given below includes a triplet subdivision of a beat or of a part of a beat. Be sure to perform the triplets evenly. A common mistake is to hurry the beginning notes of the triplet so ♩♪♪ becomes ♪♪♩ . Counteract this tendency by holding back on the first two notes.

Perform the material in the following ways:

1. Intone the pattern while conducting the meter.

2. Tap the pattern with the right hand while tapping the pulse with the left hand. Reverse hands when repeating the exercise.

3. Count the beats aloud while clapping the pattern.

Exercise VII. Ear Training

Each student is to write several phrases which include triplet sub-divisions of the pulse. After announcing the pulse note each student performs his pattern several times. The class claps the pattern and then notates it.

Exercise VIII. Drills in Compound Meter

When a composer consistently subdivides the pulse of his music into triplets he writes his music in a compound meter. The top figure of the time signature will be a multiple of 3, such as 6-9-12. When the lower number is 8 ($\frac{6}{8}$, $\frac{9}{8}$, $\frac{12}{8}$,), the pulse note is a dotted quarter-note ($\downarrow$.). When the lower number is 4 ($\frac{6}{4}$, $\frac{9}{4}$), the pulse note is a dotted half-note ($\downarrow$.). Music in which the upper figure is 6 is said to be in duple meter; when the upper figure is 9, the music is in triple meter. An upper figure of 12 shows four pulses per measure.

In quick tempos the conducting pattern is based on the pulse note so that a $\frac{6}{8}$ or $\frac{6}{4}$ gets two beats per measure. In slow tempos, particularly if the rhythmic pattern is complex, the basic conducting beat is subdivided and each subpulse is indicated. However, a sense of impulse must always be felt on the first of every group of three subpulses.

CONDUCTING PATTERNS IN SLOW COMPOUND METER

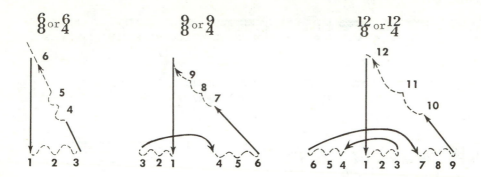

A comparatively small number of units are characteristic of compound meter. In $\frac{6}{8}$, $\frac{9}{8}$, and $\frac{12}{8}$, for example, most measures are made up of the following triplet units:

1. While tapping the basic dotted quarter-note pulse with one foot, clap each of the above units twice.

2. Clap patterns in $\frac{6}{8}$ by alternating units: 1 and 4; 1 and 5; 4 and 2; etc.

3. Clap patterns in $\frac{9}{8}$ by combining three units: 3-3-1; 10-8-6; etc.

4. Clap patterns in $\frac{12}{8}$ made by combining four units: 5-1-1-3; 4-7-11-2; etc.

5. Each student is to make up a pattern in $\frac{6}{8}$ meter by combining two basic units. The class, after several hearings of the pattern, is to decide which units were used. [notation] , for example, would be identified as units 10 and 1.

6. Many nursery rhymes are based on $\frac{6}{8}$ meter. Clap the rhythmic pattern of "Jack and Jill" and see how it is built almost exclusively on unit 3. Find the units used in other nursery rhymes. Barcarolles and gigues are usually written in compound meter. These might be played and the rhythmic units identified.

Exercise IX. Rhythmic Studies in Compound Meter

Mentally note the pulse of the dotted quarter notes while scanning each of the following studies. Make the eyes move from pulse to pulse.

1. Intone the pattern while conducting the meter (the pulse note is a dotted quarter note).

2. Intone the pattern while clapping the pulses

   (a) with the dotted quarter as the pulse note.

   (b) with the eighth note as the pulse note.

3. Tap the dotted quarter-note pulse with the right hand, the pattern with the left hand. Repeat, reversing the duties of the hands.

Exercise X. Ear Training

Invent one-measure patterns in $\frac{6}{8}$, $\frac{9}{8}$, and $\frac{12}{8}$ by combining units from the list on page 142. Dictate your measure, performing it several times. The class will then determine which units you have used. Do the same with two- and four-measure patterns.

Exercise XI. Two-part Studies in Compound Meter

Perform the patterns given below in the following ways:

1. Half the class intones the upper part, the other half intones the lower part.

2. Two soloists are chosen to perform the studies.

3. Each student intones the upper part while clapping the lower.

4. Each student taps the upper part with the right hand, the lower part with the left hand.

Canon after one beat (♩.)

The lower voice is a rhythmic ostinato.

Rhythmic canon

Exercise XII. Patterns in Six-four and Nine-four Meters

In the following patterns the quarter note is the lower figure of the time signatures for duple and triple compound meters. The dotted half note represents the pulse note, except in slow tempos, and there should be a feeling of impulse at the beginning of each group of three quarter notes. Mentally mark off the beginning of each beat, then

1. Intone the rhythm while conducting the meter.

2. Tap the pulse ($\dot{\downarrow}$) with the left hand, the rhythmic pattern with the right hand. Repeat, reversing hands.

Exercise XIII. The Tenor Clef

The *tenor clef* locates middle C on the fourth line of the staff

. As you practice the studies below, use the lines as guides,

thinking of the pitch names of each . Focus

on the fourth line (middle C) and concentrate on the spaces which surround that note (B and D). Similarly, concentrate on the spaces adjacent to the other lines of the staff.

Sing the studies below in various tempos: (a) name the pitches as they are sung; (b) use conventional syllables; (c) use scale-degree numbers; (d) use a neutral syllable.

Exercise XIV. Ear Training

Write melodies using the tenor clef, then play or sing each tune several times. After the key is announced, the class is to write each melody in the tenor clef.

Exercise XV. Excerpts from Music Literature

Perform the melodies given below while conducting the meter. Sing, using (a) scale numbers, (b) conventional syllables, and (c) a neutral syllable.

Folk song

Carol

Folk song

Andante   Beethoven

Trouvère

Purcell

Purcell

Four-part round

'Tis   wo-man makes us love.   'Tis sad-ness makes us   sad.

'Tis   sad-ness makes us drink, And drink-ing makes us mad.

Note: Many compositions that are written in $\frac{3}{4}$ or $\frac{3}{8}$ are meant to be performed in two-measure groupings so that the effect is that of a $\frac{6}{4}$ or a $\frac{6}{8}$. Such a melody is that by Weber, No. 10.

Mendelssohn

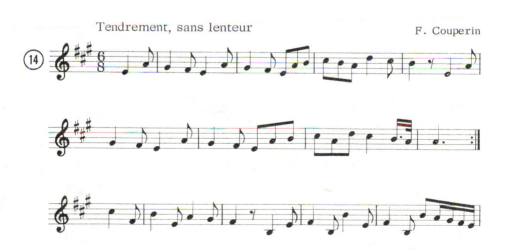

Tendrement, sans lenteur

F. Couperin

Andante   Mozart

Moderato   Handel

Bach

Bach

UNIT X

Chromatic Tones;
Melodies in Mixed Forms of the Minor Scale;
Syncopation; Excerpts from Music Literature

A *chromatic tone* used melodically may serve several purposes. It may act as a leading tone to the following tone, thereby giving greater strength to that tone; it may destroy the stability of one key and create a feeling of a new tonal center; it may be purely decorative or expressive; or it may be part of a chromatic harmony used for coloristic purposes. Chromatic tones attract attention, add color, and create melodic interest.

Melodically, the most usual types of chromatic tones are the chromatic neighboring tone and the chromatic passing tone.

Exercise I. The Chromatic Neighboring Tone

A *neighboring tone,* or *auxiliary tone,* is an embellishing tone which moves away from its generating tone and then back again. A neighboring tone may be above or below its generating tone. The lower neighboring tone is usually chromatic, except between scale degrees 3-4 and 7-8. The upper neighboring tone is usually a scale tone, although it may sometimes be a chromatic tone.

Perform the following studies on syllables and scale numbers. Note that No. 4 is based on the I-II-V₇-I harmonic progression.

UNIT X

3

4

I

II

V₇

I   V   I

5

6

7

Exercise II. The Chromatic Passing Tone

A chromatic passing tone is a tone which appears between two adjacent scale tones:

The following studies are based on ascending and descending chromatic passing tones. They should be sung with careful attention to the problem of intonation. For good intonation it is essential to think the tone to which the chromatic tone resolves.

Perform the studies on a neutral syllable and scale-degree numbers.

In using scale-degree numbers use the number of the tone as though there were no chromatic sign. Mentally note that the tone is to be raised or lowered.

D minor:

Exercise III. Melodies Using Chromaticism

The melodies given below use chromatic passing tones and neighboring tones. Scan each melody and mentally mark the chromatic tones. Sing on syllables and scale-degree numbers while conducting the meter.

Exercise IV. Ear Training

Compose a short melody which includes chromatic passing tones and auxiliary tones. Play or sing each melody several times. Announce the key, and have the class determine the meter and write the melody from dictation.

Exercise V. Melodic Studies Using Combinations
of the Various Forms of the Minor Scale

Below are further studies in the minor keys. Notice particularly the use of the sixth and the seventh degrees of the scale, reflecting the different forms of the minor scale in ascending and descending patterns. Note, too, that the ascending form of the minor scale is sometimes used in a descending pattern—as in number 6, measure 2—because of a harmonic progression.

Sing the studies while conducting the meter, using (a) scale-degree numbers, (b) conventional syllables, and (c) a neutral syllable.

Always remind yourself to look ahead when sight singing, so that you will sing in groups of notes, measures, or phrases, rather than note by note.

Exercise VI. Ear Training

Write a short melody which uses various forms of the minor scale. Sing or play your melody several times. Announce your key and then have the class sing the melody from memory, determining the meter and writing the melody.

Exercise VII. Syncopation Using Tied Notes

Syncopation is a rhythmic device in which the normal feeling of weight on strong beats or the strong part of a beat is altered. Syncopations are achieved:

(a) by omitting strong beats.

(b) by omitting strong parts of beats.

(c) by tying from a weak beat into a strong beat.

(d) by tying from a weak part of a beat into a strong part of a beat.

(e) by putting a long note, which has a feeling of weight, on a weak
     beat.

In performing syncopated patterns make a slight accent on the nor-
mally unaccented beat or weak part of the beat. Always feel the pulse
strongly so that the syncopation can be effective. If the syncopation is
within parts of beats, as in (d) above, the pulse should be thought of in
subdivisions:

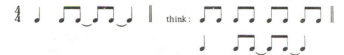

Perform the studies below in the following manner:

1. Count the beats aloud while clapping the pattern.

2. Intone the pattern while conducting the meter.

3. Tap the beat with the left hand, the pattern with the right hand. Re-
    peat, reversing the duties of the hands.

    Establish the pulse before starting. Do the patterns at various tempos.

Think in one beat per measure.

Exercise VIII. Ear Training

1. Invent some four- to six-measure rhythmic patterns, in various meters, which employ syncopations. Tap each pattern several times. Then ask the class to repeat the pattern, determine the meter, and write the rhythmic pattern.

2. Instead of inventing patterns, bring in examples of syncopation from music literature and dictate these to the class.

Exercise IX. Two-part Rhythmic Studies

Perform the following two-part rhythmic studies:

1. Half the class taps the upper part while the other half claps the lower part. Reverse parts. One student conducts the performance.

2. Two soloists perform the studies.

3. Each student taps the upper part with the right hand, the lower part with the left hand.

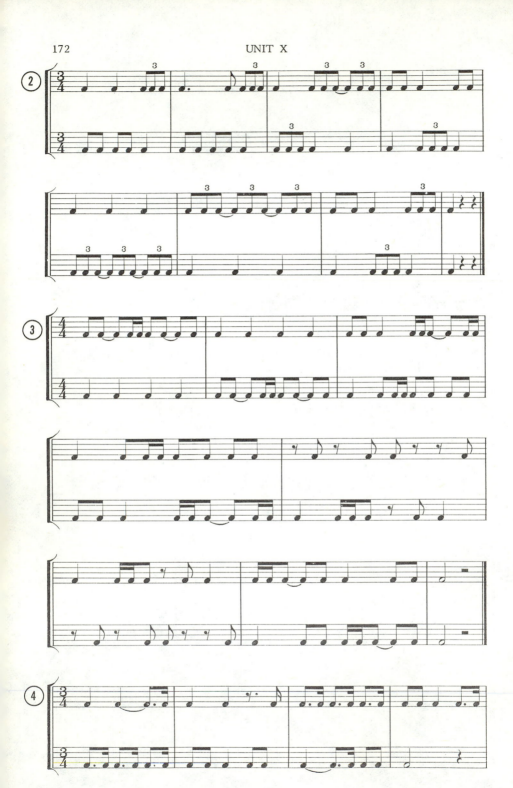

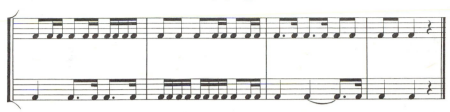

After Handel

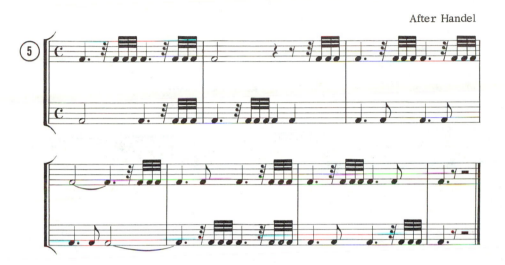

Exercise X. Excerpts from Music Literature

Sing each melody, conducting while singing. Use conventional syllables, scale-degree numbers, and a neutral syllable.

Do not stop to make corrections during the course of a phrase. If a
mistake is made, go back over the difficult passage, study it carefully,
then sing the whole phrase several times.

Train the eyes to pick out rhythmic or melodic patterns that repeat.
Be sure of the tonality before starting and keep the tonality in mind at
all times.

Allegretto   Haydn

Allegro

Handel

Handel

Mozart

*The embellishing tone should be sung on the beat and have the value of an eighth note. The pattern of the measure, then, would be: ♩ ♫ ♪ ♩ ♪.

Adagio   Mendelssohn

*These grace notes should be sung just before the beat:

Allegro non troppo   Mendelssohn

Moderato   Diabelli

Andante leggiero   Mendelssohn

Andante   Mendelssohn

Allegro moderato   Handel

Fröhlich   G. Kalkbrenner

Allegro, ma non troppo   Handel

Adagio

Allegro   Corelli

Corelli

L. Couperin

Round for three voices   T. Hilton

25 1 Turn, A - ma-ril - lis, to thy swain thy

2 Here is a pret-ty, pret-ty, pret-ty ar-bour by, where

3 here let's sit, and whilst I play,

Da - mon calls thee back a - gain;

A - pol - lo, where A - pol - lo can - not spy.

sing to my pipe a round - de - lay.

Rameau

26

Bach

Bach

UNIT XI

Accents and Cross-accents;
Leaps in Triads in Minor Keys; Tritones;
Chromaticism; Excerpts from Music Literature

Rhythmic interest in a composition is frequently obtained by having accents fall on unexpected places, such as weak beats or weaker parts of beats. Composers use such *cross-accents* to overcome obvious metric symmetry from measure to measure. There are many ways of making accents. In the following rhythmic studies they are made by putting a long note on a weak beat, as in No. 1; by seeming to put one meter against another, as in No. 7 which suggests $\frac{3}{4}$; and by the placing of an accent mark (>) or *sf* above or below a note.

Exercise 1. Accents and Cross-accents

Perform the studies in the following ways:

1. Clap the pattern while counting the beats aloud.

2. Intone the pattern while conducting the meter.

3. Tap the pattern with the right hand, the beats with the left hand. Reverse hands.

4. Subdivide each pulse into eighth notes. Tap the subdivided beats with the left hand, the pattern with the right hand. Reverse hands.

Be sure to make a distinction between accented and nonaccented notes.

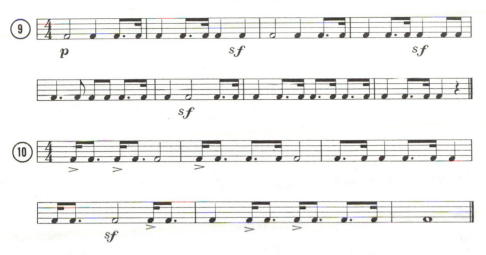

Exercise II. Ear Training

Write a rhythmic pattern, four to six measures long, employing cross-accents. After establishing the pulse and the meter, clap your pattern several times, with the proper accents. The class should repeat the pattern, then write it.

Exercise III. Leaps Within Triads in the Minor Scales

The drills given below present leaps within all the triads in the various forms of the minor scales. Some of the triads assume different aspects because of the varying ways in which the sixth and seventh scale degrees are used. However, most commonly:

> I and IV are minor triads,
> III, V, and VI are major triads,
> II and VII are diminished triads.

Sing the drills at various tempos, first mentally noting the root of each triad. Keep the basic tonality in mind. Be prepared to sing at any time the tonic and the dominant tones of the key as well as the root of the prevailing triad. Use conventional syllables, scale-degree numbers, and a neutral syllable.

III _____ IV _____ VII _____ I _____

(15)

I _____ V _____ VI _____ IV _____

II _____ I _____ VII _____ I _____

(16)

I _____ VI _____ IV _____ VII _____ I _____ II _____

III _____ IV _____ VII _____ I _____ V _____

(17)

I _____ IV _____ II _____ V _____ VI _____ VII _____

I _____ III _____ IV _____ V _____ I _____

(Compare with No. 17)

(18)

I _____ IV _____ II _____ V _____ VI _____ VII _____

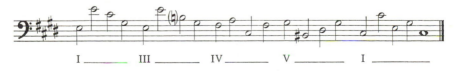

I _____ III _____ IV _____ V _____ I _____

Exercise IV. Melodic Studies Containing Tritones

The diminished triad (built on the seventh degree of the major scale and the second and seventh degrees of the *harmonic* minor scale) frequently offers difficulties in sight singing due to the melodic tritone (the diminished fifth or augmented fourth) which exists between the root and fifth of the triad. The tritone also occurs as a result of the use of chromatic tones, as in studies No. 9, 10, and 11.

Problems of intonation can be overcome if you sense in advance the tone to which the tritone ultimately resolves.

The studies given below present leaps within the diminished triad and direct leaps of the tritone.

Sing the following studies while conducting the meter, always keeping in mind the basic tonality. Use conventional syllables, scale-degree numbers, and a neutral syllable.

Exercise V. Ear Training

Write a melody, four to eight measures in length, employing tritone leaps. Announce the key and sing or play your melody several times. The class will then sing the melody, determine the meter, and write the melody.

Exercise VI.   Chromatic Studies

In the studies given below the chromatic changes are a half step or a whole step distant from the previous tone. Make the intonation of these melodies true by maintaining a sense of tonality, always keeping in mind the important scale degrees (the tones of the tonic triad).

Sing the melodies while conducting the meter. Use conventional syllables and repeat using a neutral syllable.

Exercise VII. Excerpts from Music Literature

All of the melodies given below contain a certain amount of chromaticism; some stay in the same key from beginning to end, others
modulate. Scan each melody before singing it, comparing starting tonality with the ending tonality. If there is a change of key, locate the measure, or group of measures, where the new key center begins to make
itself felt. At this point think in terms of a new tonic and dominant.

Sing each melody while conducting the meter. Use scale-degree
numbers, conventional syllables, and a neutral syllable.

Purcell

Anonymous

Polonaisenhaft   Dittersdorf

Allegro   Handel

Andante con moto   Schubert

Presto   Haydn

Andante con moto   Mendelssohn

Recitative   Mozart

Brahms

Adagio   Handel

UNIT XII

Changing Meters; Modal Music; Excerpts from Music Literature

Since the late 1800's composers have experimented with various ways of freeing rhythm from the practices of the baroque and classical periods. Some of these new techniques reflect the rhythmic freedom of Renaissance music, primitive music, and folk music; others are derived from asymmetric speech patterns and jazz syncopations. Among the different rhythmic techniques we find: changing meters

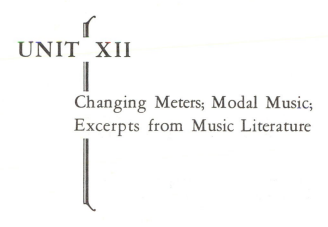

irregular meters, themselves made up of changing meters

and the use of one meter against the basic pulse of another, creating a syncopation

Exercise I. Changing Meters and Irregular Meters

The rhythmic drills given below present some of these rhythmic problems. Perform them:

1. speaking the rhythm while conducting the meter,

2. tapping or clapping the rhythm while counting aloud,

3. tapping the pulse with one hand, the pattern with the other. Reverse parts.

Make a slight accent at the beginning of each group of notes:

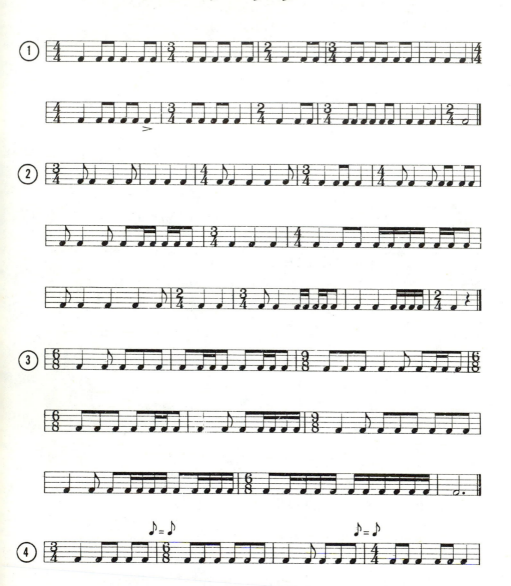

Exercise II. Ear Training

Find short melodies in which there are changes of meter or irregular meters. Play or sing your melodic examples, slightly exaggerating the measure accents. The class is to sing back the melody, determine the metric pattern, and then write the *rhythmic* pattern.

Exercise III. Modes

Music in western civilization is by no means limited to the use of the major and minor scales. Among the many scales in use the *medieval modes* play an important part. In fact, until the major-minor scale systems assumed the ascendancy in the 1600's, most music was written in the medieval church modes. For this reason a vast body of folk music is modal, reflecting its ancient lineage. Since the middle of the nineteenth century many composers, influenced by folk music, have written modal music. It is therefore important for the modern musician to be as much at home in the modes as he is in the major-minor scale systems.

Examples of the modal scales appear below.* Notice the position of the half steps. Notice, also, the relation of the tonic of the mode to the key signature: the Dorian on C has the key signature of Bb and can therefore be thought of as beginning on the second scale degree of Bb.

Sing the various modes, starting on C. Do the same with D and E as tonics.

*The Locrian mode—from B to B on the white keys on the piano—was avoided until recently by composers. It is not included in this book because of the few times it occurs in musical literature.

Exercise IV. Modal Melodies

Scan the melodies given below. Determine the mode and mentally mark the half steps. Sing the melodies, naming the pitches, using scale-degree numbers, using conventional syllables, and using a neutral syllable.

American

American

Russian

Russian

Sea Chanty

American

Irish

Exercise V. Ear Training

Find an example of a modal melody and bring it to class. Announce the starting tone and perform each melody several times. The class should determine the mode, sing the melody, and then write it.

Exercise VI. Excerpts from Music Literature

Each work should be analyzed so that any problems are identified before you attempt to sing. When there is more than one voice part, the whole class should sing each line before singing in ensemble.

Perform the examples (a) using numbers, (b) using conventional syllables, (c) using a neutral syllable, and (d) naming the pitches, if the alto clef is used.

Scott Joplin

Russian

Old English carol

Folk song

Moussorgsky

Allegro spiritoso

Mozart

Folk song

American chanty

Greek

Allegro non troppo, ma con brio   Brahms

(17)

Bach

(18)

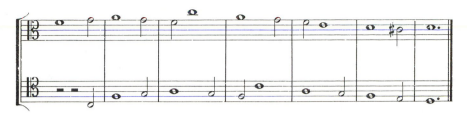

Bach

Victoria

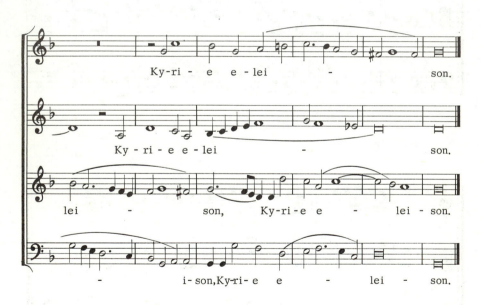

Presto

Haydn

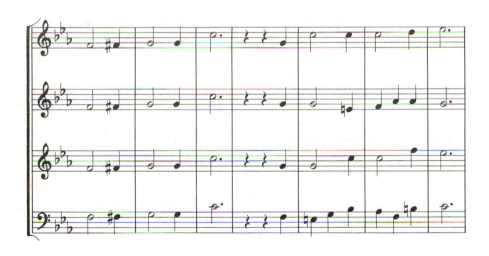

Adagio

Mozart

22

A-gnus De-i   qui tol-lis   pec-ca-ta mun-di

A-gnus De-i   qui tol-lis   pec-ca-ta mun-di

A-gnus De-i   qui tol-lis   pec-ca-ta mun-di

A-gnus De-i   qui tol-lis   pec-ca-ta mun-di

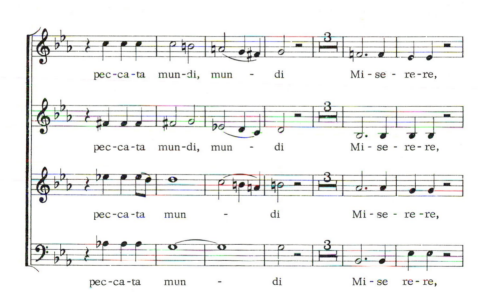

pec-ca-ta mun-di, mun - di   Mi-se - re-re,

pec-ca-ta mun-di, mun - di   Mi-se - re-re,

pec-ca-ta mun - di   Mi-se - re-re,

pec-ca-ta mun - di   Mi-se - re-re,

Mi - se - re - re no - bis,   Mi - se - re - re no - bis,

Mi - se - re - re no - bis,   Mi - se - re - re no - bis,

Mi - se - re - re no - bis,   Mi - se - re - re no - bis,

Mi - se - re - re no - bis,   Mi - se - re - re no - bis,

Mi - se - re - re, Mi - se - re - re, Mi - se - re - re no - bis.

Mi - se - re - re, Mi - se - re - re, Mi - se - re - re no - bis.

Mi - se - re - re, Mi - se - re - re, Mi - se - re - re no - bis.

Mi - se - re - re, Mi - se - re - re, Mi - se - re - re no - bis.

Printer and Binder: Halliday Lithograph

78 8 7